The WTO Agreement on Agriculture and Food Security

Christopher Stevens, Romilly Greenhill,
Jane Kennan & Stephen Devereux
Institute of Development Studies at Sussex

COMMONWEALTH SECRETARIAT

This report is part of the Commonwealth Economic Paper Series
and prepared by Christopher Stevens, Romilly Greenhill, Jane Kennan & Stephen Devereux
on behalf of the Economic Affairs Division of the Commonwealth Secretariat

Commonwealth Secretariat
Marlborough House
Pall Mall, London SW1Y 5HX, United Kingdom

Designed and published by the Commonwealth Secretariat.
Printed in Britain by Chameleon Press Limited, London.

Wherever possible, the Commonwealth Secretariat uses paper sourced from
sustainable forests or from sources that minimise a destructive impact on the environment.

ISBN 0-85092-645-9   Price: £10.99

Web site: http//www.thecommonwealth.org

Contents

Chapter 7: The Next Multilateral Agricultural Round

Chapter 8: Conclusions

Appendix 1: Identifying Vulnerable States

References

Abbreviations

ADMARC	Agriculture Development and Marketing Co-operation
AMIS	Agricultural Marketing Information Systems
AMS	Aggregate Measurement of Support
CAP	Common Agricultural Policy
EU	European Union
FAC	Food Aid Convention
FAO	Food and Agriculture Organization
GATT	General Agreement on Tariffs and Trade
GDP	Gross Domestic Product
GSP	Generalised System of Preferences
IMF	International Monetary Fund
LLDC	Least Developed Country
MFN	Most Favoured Nation
NFIDC	Net Food Importing Developing Country
NGO	Non-Governmental Organisation
OECD	Organisation for Economic Co-operation and Development
R+E	Research and Extension
SAP	Structural Adjustment Programme
SDT	Special and Differential Treatment
SME	Small and Medium Enterprise
SSA	Sub-Saharan Africa
SSG	Special Safeguards
T+V	Training and Visits Extension
TRQ	Tariff Rate Quota(s)
URAA	Uruquay Round Agreement on Agriculture
WTO	World Trade Organization

Preface

A major achievement of the Uruguay Round was the establishment of a universal framework for trade in agriculture, which means agricultural producers, exporters and trade negotiators now have a framework to work with. However, a lot remains to be done in order to bring trade in agriculture firmly within the rules of the multilateral trading system. This includes work related to further clarification of the rules governing agricultural trade and the removal of perceived asymmetries in the current agreement. Of particular concern to many developing countries with large populations engaged in small scale agriculture, mostly of a subsistence type, is the treatment to be given to their food security concerns in future multilateral trade negotiations on agriculture.

This report provides a well-researched view of the food security concerns of developing countries and how they are likely to be affected by future multilateral trade liberalisation of agriculture. The report is the product of a collaborative effort among three institutions: the Department for International Development (DFID), which funded the report; the Institute of Development Studies (IDS) at Sussex, whose experts were responsible for researching and writing the report; and the Commonwealth Secretariat, responsible for publishing and distributing the report. Preparation of the terms of reference and comments on earlier drafts of the report were coordinated by DFID.

The report identifies some of the key issues in the debate. It is a contribution from the three organisations to the growing realisation that the food security concerns of developing countries deserve serious consideration in any future multilateral trade negotiations on agriculture.

Rumman Faruqi
Director, Economic Affairs Division
Commonwealth Secretariat

Executive Summary

This report deals with an area of overlap between two large areas of study: on livelihoods and food security, and on international trade and policy. Whilst it concentrates on one small element of each of these broad areas (and so ignores many questions), it does so for a good reason. This is to avoid the danger that the upcoming WTO agricultural negotiations fail to contribute as strongly as they might to the promotion of food security precisely because the two areas of work and study overlap only at the margins.

What is Food Security?

Food (in)security is primarily a phenomenon relating to individuals, and is determined by three sets of factors concerned with supply, access and guarantees to food. In the multilateral world, by contrast, the issue is much narrower. Food security is considered as a state affair, and discussion tends to focus on adequate supplies of imported food. To widen the discussion, the entitlements approach has been used to identify the various ways in which international trade might impinge upon individual food security and, by analogy, to identify the characteristics that would tend to make some countries more food insecure than others.

Food security may be said to be determined by:
- production-based entitlements, which will be influenced by policies that affect the demand and supply of factors affecting production, some of which will relate to international trade;

- trade-based entitlements, which will be influenced by policies that affect the level and variability of food prices in relation to the price of what individuals are able to exchange for food; in cases where there are substantial agricultural exports, trade-based entitlements are likely to be affected by policy on both sides of the trade balance;

- labour-based entitlements, which are influenced by the level and location of employment opportunities which may, in turn, be influenced by trade policy;

- transfer-based entitlements, which include formal transfers from governments and aid donors that may be influenced by multilateral trade agreements.

Food Insecure States

By analogy, the food security of a state can be said to depend upon:
- its production entitlements, which reflect the food that can be produced domestically;

- its trade entitlements, which reflect its ability to earn sufficient foreign exchange with exports to purchase imported food; and

- its transfer entitlements, which cover food that can be obtained either directly through food aid or indirectly by (semi-) commercial imports financed through financial aid.

Food insecure states are those where both production and trade entitlements are problematic: the country's agricultural production is insufficient or too irregular to guarantee adequate supplies every year, and export revenue is not sufficiently strong to give confidence that, regardless of world market conditions, food could be imported to make up any shortfall without severe consequences for other import-dependent areas. (It may be assumed that any state that is dependent upon transfer entitlements for an adequate supply is food insecure, since aid is intrinsically unreliable in the medium term.)

In order to illustrate some common characteristics of food insecure states, three criteria have been derived from this analysis. They relate to GDP, vulnerability and dependence on imported food. A group of 17 states has been compiled, together with a reference group of three others. Between them, they exemplify the differing interests of developing countries in international agricultural trade.

Multilateral Policies and Food Security

Government policy is only one influence on entitlements, and the subset described specifically as 'food security policies' represents only one part of the picture. It is, nonetheless, an important part. Entitlements identified can be promoted or protected by a wide range of government interventions. These include measures to promote food production, facilitate the operations of markets, enhance the availability and value of labour entitlements, and provide transfers and safety nets. In addition, enabling macro and sectoral policies will have an indirect effect on food security.

Multilateral trade negotiations may affect this pattern of government action in two ways:

❖ by introducing change to the policies (of both domestic and foreign governments) that impact directly on entitlements (for example, by altering the food prices paid by consumers or received by producers);

❖ by making more or less feasible some of the policies that are considered desirable to promote or protect entitlements.

The multilateral policy areas most likely to affect entitlement protection and promotion policies are those on:

❖ tariffs (which could affect government revenue and, in this way, impact on many policies);

❖ domestic subsidies (which could alter the feasibility of policies related to production and transfer entitlements);

❖ export subsidies (which could affect the feasibility of transfer and safety net policies).

In addition, multilateral rules on state trading enterprises and export regulation, as well as any new rules on process criteria, could have an impact.

The Impact of the Uruguay Round

The changes agreed in the Uruguay Round Agreement on Agriculture (URAA) had the potential to affect food security in two ways. First, there are restrictions placed upon the policy freedom of governments; these might be called 'direct effects'. Certain policies that have been used in the past, or might be proposed for the future, may not now be available to governments. These effects are fairly easy to identify precisely.

The second type of effect, which could be called 'indirect effects', may be more substantial in the longer term but are much more difficult to identify precisely. One impact of the direct effects will be to alter world market conditions for agriculture. This is likely to provoke changes in both the level and the distribution of supply and demand. This will, in turn, alter the prices that some countries receive for their exports and pay for their imports.

On most counts these effects have not been sufficiently substantial to influence food security. The provisions of the URAA did not 'bite' in this sense. Nonetheless, the potential remains: there have been both direct and indirect effects of the Round and, by establishing the architecture for future negotiations, it may have a much greater medium-term impact if the forthcoming multilateral negotiations produce more substantial change.

The overall effects of the URAA on food security policies are summarised in the table below. This takes the types of useful food security policies identified in Part 2 of the report (column 1), identifies the part of the URAA's architecture that is most relevant to their feasibility (column 2), and then specifies the provisions in the URAA that may be used to support such policies, distinguishing between those most and least used by developing countries. Those food security policies that involve direct government subsidies (such as input credits and food price stabilisation) can be pegged on the special and differential treatment

(SDT) and *de minimis* exemptions. Hence they have not been adversely affected to any substantial extent by the URAA. The role of tariffs in providing some degree of protection to domestic producers and government revenue (*inter alia* for food security expenditure) has also been maintained by the large amount of 'water' in developing country bound rates. The direct impact on feeding programmes of the URAA cuts in the subsidised exports of (mainly) developed countries has been small, but since it has occurred in the context of sharp falls in food aid the pain may have been greater than would appear from the aggregate figures.

Table 1 Provisions relating to food security in the URAA

Food security policies	Related WTO trade policy area	URAA provisions available to developing countries		URAA effect
		Widely used	*Not widely used*	
Input credits and subsidies; capital expenditure in agriculture; food price stabilisation and subsidies	Domestic subsidies	SDT exemptions from cuts in agricultural investment and input subsidies for poor farmers 10% *de minimis* exemption LLDCs exempt from any cuts	Green Box Substantial base AMS	Limited
All policies involving government expenditure; export development; protection to domestic farmers	Tariffs	High bound rates containing 'water' Lower (for developing) and zero (for least developed) tariff cutting obligations	SSGs TRQs	Limited
Labour-intensive public works and targeted feeding programmes; food stamps	Export subsidies	Food aid exempt from developed country reduction commitments		Limited but relatively important for vulnerable states in context of food aid cutback

At the same time, it is clear that there are several other substantial pegs on which food security policies might have been justified, but which are not usable in practice by developing countries that failed to take the necessary steps during the URAA. This is not a problem for food security – provided that the pegs available to developing countries remain adequate for the task. But they could become inadequate in future unless a new agreement either confirms their retention or provides alternatives.

The Next Agricultural Round

All of the main sources of food security entitlement could be affected by the next agricultural trade Round, which, as noted above, may introduce change to the policies that impact directly on the level of entitlements or alter the feasibility of some of the policies that are considered desirable to promote or protect entitlements.

Current expectations are that the next agricultural trade Round will cover three main areas – export subsidies, market access and domestic subsidies. All three have the potential to impinge upon food security either:

❖ directly, by establishing new rules on food security policies currently in place or recommended in vulnerable developing countries; or

❖ indirectly, by altering absolute and relative agricultural prices which will, in turn, change entitlements.

These three areas have been listed in the order in which most change is anticipated. But in terms of the likely impact on food security, the priority order is different. It is domestic subsidies, tariffs and export subsidies.

There is thus an asymmetry between the areas likely to have the greatest impact on food security and those anticipated, at present, to feature most prominently in the negotiations. One consequence is that positive effects cannot simply be assumed to result (for example from

developed country liberalisation), but another is that it ought to be feasible to identify modalities that will prevent serious adverse effects. The prime requirement for this second outcome is that negotiators are informed about the implications of proposed change for the entitlements of the food insecure.

The conclusion from this study is that there is no overwhelming reason to suppose that it will be difficult to achieve a balance in the new rules between the desirable objectives of extending robust disciplines to international trade in temperate agricultural products and fostering sensible food security policies. Given the uncertainty over the negotiating agenda, let alone the extent to which agreement can be reached, it is not possible to make any estimate of the potential effects of the next Round. But a number of desirable guidelines can be identified.

❖ Developing countries should have sufficient time and support to introduce alternative revenue sources.

❖ The erosion of rents in protected OECD markets in which developing countries receive preferences should be achieved principally by increased market access rather than through cuts in administered prices. This is because enhanced access for imports would tend to reduce prices in the protected market (by increasing supply relative to demand), but would do so in a way that allowed efficient exporters to increase sales. Cuts in administered prices without market opening, by contrast, simply result in a revenue loss to the favoured exporters without any beneficial shift in the international division of labour.

❖ The production and trade entitlements of farmers should be protected from dumped imports. The means by which this is to be achieved is less important than the objective.

- The URAA established a distinction in SDT between developing countries and the least developed sub-group. But the latter is not an entirely satisfactory category for identifying food insecure states. If SDT for the broader category of developing countries is reduced, a new sub-category of food insecure states may be desirable.

- The institutional asymmetry between provisions for developed and developing country subsidies should be resolved in a way that recognises that it is often desirable from the perspective of food security to have production-related government support in insecure states.

Part 1

The Foundations
Chapter 1: Introduction

1.1 The Aims of the Study

This study aims to help identify how a future multilateral agreement on agricultural trade can provide a secure framework within which developing countries can pursue effective policies to ensure their food security.[1] Burgeoning international agricultural trade has a growing impact on the food security of individuals, households and communities. Because of this international agricultural trade policy does have a role to play in food security, even though its importance should not be exaggerated relative to domestic arrangements or international trade policy for industrial products and services.

1.2 What is Food Security?

This report deals with an area of overlap between two large areas of study: those, on the one hand, of livelihoods and food security, and, on the other, international trade and policy. It concentrates on one small element of each of these broad areas of study, and in so doing ignores many of the questions and issues that preoccupy specialists on food security and on international trade policy.

The reason for this focus is to avoid the danger that the upcoming WTO agricultural negotiations fail to contribute as strongly as they might to the promotion of food security precisely because the two areas of work and study overlap only at the margins. Those concerned with issues of livelihoods and food security are not always attuned to the ways in which changing trade policy could have an effect (for example by making favoured approaches less feasible or unfavourable tendencies more likely). On the other side, since international trade negotiations are between states, whereas food security is primarily an individual or group concern, they may fail to consider the multiple, overlapping ways in which food security may be affected, with the result that is exemplified by the tendency to equate food security with national agricultural import capacity.

The very broad range of factors that affect the sustainability of livelihoods is illustrated in Figure 1, which has been produced to establish the parameters for the analysis of rural livelihoods. The forthcoming WTO negotiations impact upon this complex picture primarily as one of several factors influencing just one part of the table: that relating to the terms of trade. Together with the technical and market influences on terms of trade, policy change will influence the relative prices of a range of agricultural outputs and inputs. In so doing, it will make some existing activities less feasible than they currently are and will make others more feasible. This is bound to have differential effects not only between countries but also between social and gender groups within states. It is to the nature of such changes that this report is addressed.

---

1   The study was funded by DFID. The conclusions are solely those of the authors.

Figure 1 Sustainable rural livelihoods: a framework for analysis

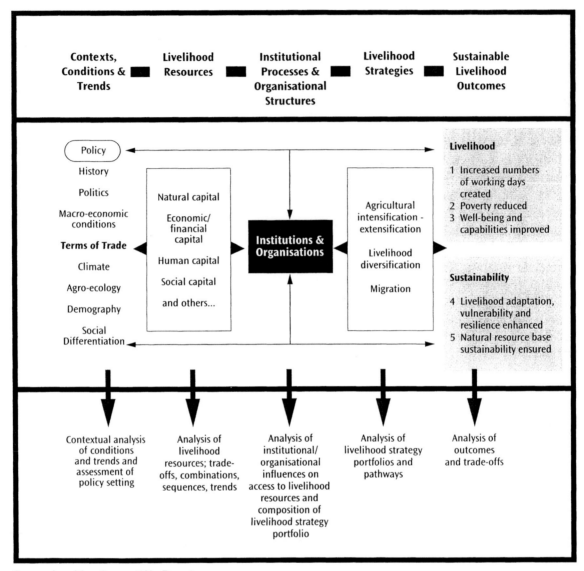

Source: adapted from Scoones 1998a: Figure 1.

1.2.1 At the individual level

The concept of food security as used in this study is a broad one. Food security has been defined in many different ways at different times and by different institutions [Maxwell 1990]. The most widely accepted definition of food security at the individual level is that of the World Bank: 'Secure access by all people at all times to enough food for a healthy, active life' [IBRD 1986]. This includes the three elements that are widely agreed to be necessary for food security:

❖ *enough* food for an active healthy life;

❖ *access* to this food; and

❖ the *guarantee* of having access to it at any given time [Christiaensen 1995].

1.2.2 At the national level

At the national level, the evolving food security debate during the 1970s and 1980s made clear what is obvious at the individual level: national food security does not require individual countries to achieve food production self-sufficiency. Depending on a country's factor endowments, a more lucrative and perhaps even safer option might be to produce and export high-value crops or manufactured goods, and to purchase some proportion of national staple food requirements on world markets. Conversely, countries can be food self-sufficient at the national level but also contain some food insecure individuals because of unequal distribution of food within the country. This distinction between self-sufficiency and food security at the national level is demonstrated in Table 2.

Table 2 Food security and self-sufficiency

	Food secure	Food insecure
Food self-sufficient	USA	Myanmar
Not food self-sufficient	Norway Japan Singapore	Malawi

1.2.3 At the multilateral level

Within the context of the WTO, the term 'food security' is used in a different, narrower sense. It is often taken to relate primarily to the adequate supply of imported food to member states. This reflects concern that the liberalisation of world agricultural trade could lead to a rise in world prices for commercial imports and a reduction in the volume of food aid available. The nature of the issues conveyed by the term food security is well summed up in the title and content of the Uruguay Round *Decision on Measures Concerning the Possible Negative Effects of the Reform Programme on Least Developed and Net Food-importing Developing Countries* and in Article 16 of *The Agreement on Agriculture*.

1.2.4 The approach of the study

As is clear from the preferred definition, this study has cast the net of food security much more widely than is common in multilateral trade discussions. Not only does it consider a wider range of policy instruments than those concerned with the price and availability of imported food, but it also establishes that food security is primarily an individual and community affair rather than a concern of states. Although some states are poorer and more vulnerable than others, it is primarily individuals that are food (in)secure.

While the objective of the study is to identify ways in which multilateral trade liberalisation could affect food security policies, this broader approach to the concept of food security suggests that it is desirable to place the analysis within the wider context of the ways in which security is enhanced or reduced. There are many factors affecting an individual's food (in)security other than the influence of government actions described as *food security policies*.

1.3 Organisation of the Report

In order to combine this broad treatment with precise conclusions on the potential relationship between liberalisation and food security *policies*, the report is divided into three main parts.

❖ **Part 1** explains the concept of food security, its determinants and their relationship to trade. Using the analytical framework of Sen's entitlement approach, it illustrates the different ways in which food security can be achieved. It then shows analytically the ways in which changes to trade policy could impact upon these sources of entitlements. Finally, it summarises the ways in which agricultural trade may affect food security.

❖ **Part 2** applies the findings of Part 1 to policies. It focuses attention on food security *policies*, reviewing the literature on entitlement promotion and protection policies to establish the ones considered to be most cost effective. It then identifies those that could be affected by multilateral agricultural trade liberalisation.

❖ **Part 3** assesses the effects of the URAA against the benchmarks established in Parts 1 and 2. It then analyses the potential scope of the next Round of multilateral negotiations to have an impact on food security policies.

Chapter 2: The Entitlements Approach to Food Security

This chapter places the subject of this study in its wider context by presenting the findings of a literature review on food security. This has been designed to highlight those factors most likely to be affected directly or indirectly by trade liberalisation.

It uses the entitlements approach as an organising framework within which the determinants of food security can be analysed. The entitlements approach was first developed by Sen in 1981, replacing earlier theories which stressed shortages in food availability as causes of food insecurity. In contrast, Sen's approach focuses on household access to food, or 'entitlements'.

Sen suggested that entitlement relations 'connect one set of ownerships to another through certain rules of legitimacy' [1986:1]. He identified four types of entitlement relationships:

❖ production-based entitlements, which entail that individuals are entitled to what they produce;

❖ trade-based entitlements, entailing that people are entitled to what they can obtain by selling or bartering physical assets (including livestock and cash crops);

❖ labour-based entitlements, meaning that people are entitled to what they can obtain through the sale of their labour power; and

❖ transfer-based entitlements which mean that an individual is entitled to what is given to them through legal transfer, be it formal (from government) or informal (from friends and relatives).

For the purposes of this study, the entitlements framework is useful even though it has been critiqued by various authors for neglecting the underlying structural causes of food insecurity [Devereux 1993], and for downplaying the relationship between poverty and food insecurity [Stewart 1982, cited in Devereux 1993]. It analyses the interactions between different sources of entitlement, and the extent to which risks are correlated across them. The four categories are exhaustive in that they describe all legal means of securing food. The first two will be impacted upon directly by multilateral trade agreements, while the fourth could be affected via changes to government tariff revenue and the cost/availability of food imports.

The chapter analyses the determinants of the different sources of entitlements. It illustrates both the potential of liberalisation to affect food security and that the scale (and even direction) of any such effects can be influenced by a range of other factors. This explains why it is often so difficult to draw direct lines of causality from changes to trade policy to changes in food security status.

2.1 Production-Based Entitlements

For the majority of poor people in developing countries, the most important determinant of production-based entitlements is access to productive assets such as land, trees or livestock, on the basis of either ownership or other rights – for example, usufruct rights over land. While in the short run these are likely to be reasonably fixed, in the long run they may change as a result of policies such as land reform and household investment decisions. Investment, in turn, will be affected by the price levels and variability of what is produced, which may be affected by trade policy. Prices are important to provide both incentives and finance to undertake investments. Off-farm employment to provide cash to finance investments and/or access to credit will also affect investment decisions. In turn, government non-trade policies, for example as a result of SAPs, may affect access to credit. For example, credit ceilings have resulted in some cases in reduced access to credit, especially for poorer producers.

Production-based entitlements will also be affected by household access to agricultural inputs such as fertilisers and seeds. This will be influenced by price and availability of these inputs which, in turn, may be affected by liberalisation. Government policies may also have an impact on the price of inputs through subsidies and price controls, and on availability through the actions of parastatals.

Technology will also impact upon the level of production and thus production-based entitlements. Provision of research and extension will impact upon technology adoption decisions. Again, overall budgetary considerations, for example as a result of structural adjustment policies, may influence the provision of research and extension.

Finally, health and climatic/environmental factors have been identified in the literature as impacting upon production. Health affects production via the productivity of labour. Policy variables, such as government expenditure and the provision of health services in the rural areas, are one determinant of health. Some climatic and environmental factors are also affected by policy changes, although others – such as rainfall – will be largely out of policy control.

2.2 Trade-Based Entitlements

Except for households that are entirely self-sufficient in all their food needs (an increasingly rare category), access to food through the market is an important component of household food security.

The main factor affecting trade-based entitlements is the level and variability of the price of food relative to whatever individuals are able to exchange for it. Retail food prices at a point in time and their variability over time will in turn depend on a number of factors.

❖ The **total supply of food**, as determined by production and imports is an important, but not the only, factor.

❖ The degree of **market integration** (determined by infrastructure and marketing), will affect the extent to which changes in production or imports are transmitted into price changes in different areas.

❖ **Government price controls** and/or subsidies, where they exist, will have an effect. The access of individuals to food at these subsidised or controlled prices is also important. (Price controls may also adversely affect the trade-based entitlements of producers.)

❖ If food is imported, entitlements will be affected by **global supply and demand** (which, in turn, will be determined partly by the policies of other countries), the exchange rate, and the importing state's trade policies.

❖ **Transport costs** (domestic and international) are important, and will be determined *inter alia* by infrastructure and the existence and performance of marketing agents, whether private or public.

The extent of entitlements will also be affected by the price of what consumers have to sell, which in the case of those engaged in farming is also linked to agricultural markets. While related to market levels, the prices actually received by producers will depend on the additional factors noted above. Particularly important is the existence and performance of **marketing agents.**

There is a general agreement in the literature that:

❖ government parastatals have often been highly inefficient and thus have paid producers lower prices than could have been paid in a more efficient system; but that

❖ in order for the private sector to replace government parastatals, supportive policies – for example, the provision of credit and infrastructure – must also be in place.

Regulations which restrict the actions of private traders – for example, prohibitions on the transport of food across different areas – have also been found to affect food security negatively. Concerns have also been raised that private traders may not serve higher-cost areas. Such high-cost areas may be those with poor infrastructure, and thus precisely those areas in which the food insecure are most likely to be located. Individual private traders are less willing and able than national parastatals to cross-subsidise loss-making markets with profits earned elsewhere, which suggests that a scaled down (but not abolished) grain marketing parastatal might retain an important food security function even after its commercial activities have been privatised.

If production is exported, the price will be affected by the exchange rate, world prices and the access that exporters have to external markets, which are in turn affected by policies pursued in other countries. Price variability on international markets may also affect price variations domestically, depending on the extent to which international price changes are fed through into changes in producer prices.

The variability of food prices will also depend on the variability of production and the extent to which production shortfalls are met by imports, as well as the degree of market integration. If food is imported, the variability of prices on international markets will also affect the variability of food prices domestically unless offset by government policy.

2.3 Labour-Based Entitlements

Labour-based entitlements will be influenced by both the level and the location of employment opportunities. These will be affected in turn by overall macroeconomic policy, particularly as it affects employment generation. The rate and structure of economic growth, which will impact upon labour-based entitlements, will be determined *inter alia* by the opportunities for export and the incomes earned therefrom, which in turn will be influenced by trade barriers in major export markets, world prices and exchange rates. Non-trade policies are also likely to impact upon employment and thus labour-based entitlements. In particular, labour and minimum wage legislation will have a major effect.

In rural areas, employment opportunities on larger farms will also affect labour-based entitlements. It has been suggested in the literature that, as larger farms are often exporters, export prices will feed through into increased rural employment generation and thus increase labour-based entitlements. Higher incomes on exporting farms can also increase revenues for rural enterprises which often have high income elasticities of demand.

Labour-based entitlements will also be affected by the labour power, technical knowledge and skills embodied in different individuals and households, which will be affected by the provision of health and education, and also by nutrition and food security. All will be influenced by the rate of population growth.

2.4 Transfer-Based Entitlements

Transfers differ from other entitlement categories because they are not produced or earned directly by the individual but are donated by others. Formal transfers come from the state, aid donors or NGOs, while informal transfers come from relatives and friends. Formal transfers will clearly depend on government policies: the existence and extent of transfers of cash or food will affect transfer-based entitlements. The existence and strength of social networks, including kinship networks, is an important determinant of informal transfers, as is the extent to which risks are correlated across kinship networks. Any impact of international trade would tend to be indirect, via its effects on social structure (to strengthen or weaken the effectiveness of informal networks) and on government revenue (to change the scope for public provision).

Chapter 3: The Impact of Trade Policy on Food Security

3.1 The International Environment

3.1.1 The growing importance of trade

Although international trade is only one of the factors affecting the food security of a country/socio-economic group/individual, its absolute importance is increasing. This is because world trade in food has grown extremely rapidly. World cereal imports in the mid-1990s, for example, were almost three times the level of those in the early 1960s. The increase has been spread over all developing regions, with North Africa, sub-Saharan Africa (SSA), Asia and Latin America/Caribbean all seeing their share of this growing total rise over the period 1961 – 96.

Although food aid has played a part in the growth in imports (especially in SSA), it is less important (indeed, much less important in most regions) than commercial imports (see Figure 2). As in other areas, the world has become more integrated, with a growing number of people in developing countries relying for part of their food intake on international trade.

Figures requested for *The WTO Agreement on Agriculture and Food Security*

Figure 2. Cereals imports and food aid, 1970–96 *(million metric tons)*

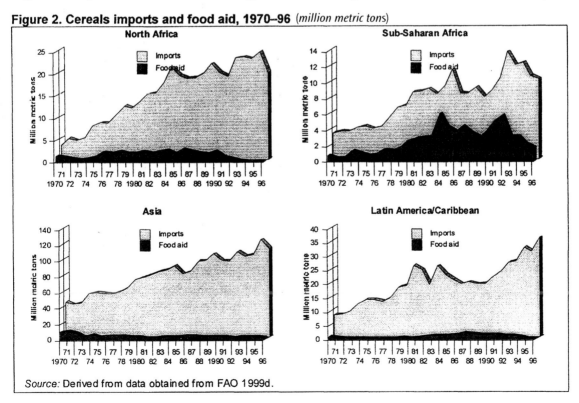

Source: Derived from data obtained from FAO 1999d.

This trend has some clear benefits, but it also raises the danger that changes to global supply and demand could have significant effects on food security. Such changes are likely to occur as a result of agricultural trade policy reform. This is because the current pattern, and scale, of supply and demand has been influenced significantly by the agricultural policy distortions that have arisen (especially in developed countries) in the absence of strong multilateral rules.

The absence until the URAA of robust disciplines for international agricultural trade is both the cause and effect of the substantial and complex distortions that exist in the agricultural markets of most OECD states. The complicated nature of these, and their long duration, mean that the task of identifying their net effect, and hence the consequences of their removal, is fraught with difficulty. It is reasonable to suppose that patterns of production throughout the world are different from what they would have been under a liberal trade regime. Hence the adjustment to liberalisation could involve quite unexpected changes in consumption and production patterns.

Whilst it is difficult to identify empirically the likely effects of liberalisation, it is more straightforward to chart the ways in which current distortions have affected world markets. From this, the cross-cutting and offsetting effects of liberalisation on different countries and groups within them can be inferred even if the scale of the effect remains an area for speculation.

3.1.2 The effects of OECD protectionism

The broad effects of agricultural protectionism (like other forms of protectionism) are the same wherever they are practised. However, developed country protectionism tends to figure prominently in analyses of world agricultural markets because of the combination of:

❖ very substantial levels of market interference;

❖ the substantial share of both world consumption and production accounted for by developed countries.

This sub-section identifies several of the ways in which developing countries' food security might have been affected by past distortions and, by implication, future liberalisation. The next sub-section reviews the findings of econometric studies that have attempted to simulate the quantitative effect of liberalisation. Whilst these are speculative, they do provide an order of magnitude of the anticipated effects.

The most fundamental effect is via the impact of developed country protectionism on the volume and distribution of global production. But there are additional effects that arise from the modalities of protection and, especially, the combination of these with trade policy on preferences. Table 3 identifies four potential effects on developing countries of the complex distortions created by protection and preferences.

Global supply and demand

The most fundamental effect of developed country protectionism has been its impact on world supply. There is widespread agreement that it has increased the levels of global production but may have depressed demand in the protected markets. This results in world prices being lower than they would otherwise have been. This, in turn, produces differential effects on net exporters and importers.

❖ Exporters lose revenue through:
  • absence from protected markets;
  • lower prices in markets that are not protected;
  • subsidised competition for some products.

❖ Importers gain revenue through:
  • lower import prices.

Table 3 Effects of agricultural protectionism on developing countries

Type of effect	Positive features	Negative features	Implications for food security policy
Increased world supply	Lowers import costs for importers (and may increase supply of food aid)	Lowers export prices for exporters Disincentive to agricultural development of importers and exporters	May undermine agricultural development policies, but also reduces food costs
Artificially high OECD prices	Artificially high prices for developing countries able to export (e.g. because of Lomé Protocols)	Exports may be viable only if high prices continue	May support export diversification, but new exports may be unsustainable
Over-subsidised prices of exports	Lowers import costs for importers	May undermine domestic agriculture and disrupt legitimate trade	May undermine agricultural development policies
Increased world price instability		Increases food insecurity and complicates agricultural development planning	Disrupts long-term agricultural development

In both groups of countries there is a tendency for agricultural production to be depressed. The effects on *groups within states* will depend partly upon their status as consumers or producers of competitive products, but also on the policies of their governments. There is a range of interventions that importing governments can undertake that will offset any negative effects of, for example, increased competition from subsidised developed country exports on domestic production. These include maintaining tariffs at a level that offsets the subsidy, using countervailing duties, or providing incentives to domestic producers. The scope for taking these actions under the URAA and its successor is examined in Part 3.

Protectionism and preferences

One of the fundamental mechanisms through which developed countries have supported their farmers is by restricting supply on to the domestic market in order to maintain prices at higher levels than otherwise would apply. This has had effects that, when combined with trade preferences, are additional to those arising from the impact on world supply.

Trade preferences can have a very important effect in relation to products controlled in this way. These take the form of:

❖ special quotas (known as tariff rate quotas – TRQs) that allow some third parties to supply the protected high-priced market without paying the substantial import duties that either exclude other imports or reduce drastically their profitability (e.g. the Lomé Beef and Sugar Protocols, which provide highly preferential access for a quota set in relation to each beneficiary);

❖ preferences that relieve some third parties from a part of the price maintenance provisions and therefore increase their ability to compete with less-favoured imports (e.g. the tariff reductions on fruit and vegetables available under Lomé, the Super GSP and most bilateral agreements).

The effect of the combined import restriction and preference is to limit the volume of imports (thereby maintaining prices) but to discriminate in favour of some suppliers at the expense of others. The impact of these changes on any given country depends both on its preferential status and on its ability to increase competitive supply. In some cases, developing countries gain more on the 'swings' of high prices than they lose on the 'roundabouts' of restricted volumes.

Dumping

Developed countries, and especially the EU, have been accused of disrupting domestic agricultural production and trade in some developing country regions not just through the general effect on supply but through specific instances of extremely low-priced exports. The market effects of administered export subsidies are more severe than those of general producer subsidies. Not only are some exports sold at less than the cost of production in the exporter (which is presumably a normal state of affairs), but also some may be sold at less than the cost of production anywhere in the world. These exports are dumped in the fullest sense of the word.

The implication is that other exporters cannot compete on world markets unless they are able to match the subsidies. For importing countries, the impact depends upon whether it is consumers or domestic producers that are being considered. Evidently, consumers benefit from the subsidies paid by developed country taxpayers. But, unless the importing government adopts appropriate policies (such as the application of a countervailing duty), domestic producers are likely to be unable to compete with the artificially cheap imports, even though they may be globally competitive and the country may have a comparative advantage in that item.

3.1.3 Estimates of the impact

There have been a large number of partial and general equilibrium studies designed to simulate the effect of liberalisation on world prices. This sub-section reviews the findings of some of the more recent.

Econometric studies on the impact of OECD agricultural policies on world prices have come to very differing conclusions, reflecting their commodity and geographical scope, the assumptions made and the time period selected.

Studies undertaken during the Uruguay Round negotiations focused on the world price changes to be expected from substantial OECD liberalisation. Three studies give the following range of price changes as a result of full OECD liberalisation: wheat: 5 – 27%; coarse grains: -10% to 22%; meat 5 – 40%; dairy products 14 – 84%; and sugar 6 – 57% [Goldin and Knudsen 1990; UNCTAD/WIDER 1990; Anderson and Tyers 1991, cited in Page et al. 1991].

The most recent studies have attempted to estimate the world price effects of the anticipated and actual results of the URAA. The results of five of these studies are summarised in Table 4. They are likely to overstate the effects of the agreement, possibly by a substantial margin. This is because they are based on simulations, carried out before the details of the final agreement were known. They assume a more substantial degree of liberalisation than was actually achieved. The actual Uruguay Round agreement implies liberalisation that is in the order of 20% (compared with the 30 – 50% assumed by four of the five studies in Table 4). This implies that the figures in Table 4 should be reduced by one-third [Pryke and Woodward 1994].

Table 4 Estimated effects of the GATT agreement on world prices for temperate agricultural products (% change from counterfactual simulation[a])

Authors	% liberal-isation	Effect on world prices (%):						
		Wheat	Coarse grains	Sugar	Veg. oils	Soya	Beef	Dairy prods
Goldin, Knudsen & van der Mensbrugghe 1993	30	+5.9	+3.6	+10.2	+4.1	n/a	+4.7	+7.2
Goldin & van der Mensbrugghe 1992	30	-0.4	+2.3	+9.3	+2.7	n/a	+4.0 [b]	+6.0
Brown and Goldin 1992	10	+4.0	-0.1	+1.5	n/a	-0.3	+0.9	n/a
Brown and Goldin 1992	50	+2.0	-0.3	+7.6	n/a	-1.5	+4.9	n/a
Page, Davenport & Hewitt 1991	33	+7	+1.8	+5.0	n/a	n/a	+5.3	+9.3

Notes: (a) Change from the situation in the absence of the GATT agreement.
　　　　(b) Beef, veal and sheep-meat.
Source: adapted from Pryke and Woodward 1994.

3.2 Vulnerable States
3.2.1 Food security and states

It was established in Chapter 2 that the definition of food (in)security used normally in the multilateral arena is more restricted in scope than that applied in the entitlements literature, but that the latter refers primarily to individuals and households, not states. It is necessary to find some means of translating the concept from the individual to the national level because:

❖　WTO negotiations are between states and affect national trade-related policy;

❖　it is desirable to use the broader definition of food security.

States can be considered by analogy to acquire food like individuals through various entitlements, of which the production, trade and transfer components translate fairly easily to the national level:

❖　the production entitlements of a country reflect the food that can be produced domestically;

❖　the trade entitlements reflect the ability

of the country to earn sufficient foreign exchange with exports to purchase imported food; and

❖　the transfer entitlements cover food that can be obtained either directly through food aid or indirectly by (semi-) commercial imports financed through financial aid.

Just as food supply is only one of the elements determining an individual's food security, so *agricultural* trade policy is only one factor at the state level. Farmers may choose to achieve food security through the cultivation of high-value crops for export, for example, rather than the production of food for self-sufficiency. Urban workers and their dependants may achieve food security through participating in international trade in manufactures. It follows that the focus of this study is just one part of a much broader picture: food security policies are only an aspect of the food security scene; agricultural trade is only one element of the impact of international commerce on food security; and trade more generally is only one of the factors involved in establishing an individual's food (in)security.

With this caveat, one could identify food insecure states as being those where both production and trade entitlements are problematic: the country's agricultural production is insufficient or too irregular to guarantee adequate supplies every year, and export revenue is not sufficiently strong to give confidence that, regardless of the state of the world market, food could be imported to make up any shortfall without severe consequences for other import-dependent areas. (It may be assumed that any state that is dependent upon transfer entitlements for an adequate supply is food insecure, since aid is intrinsically unreliable in the medium term.)

This suggests that the most food insecure states are those that combine inadequate domestic production with an export structure that is unsatisfactory in terms of one or more of the following characteristics: low *per capita* value, poor growth prospects, heavy dependence upon a small number of commodities facing fluctuating supply or demand, or heavy reliance of exports on a single market with fluctuating demand. Neither low GDP nor dependence upon imported food are, by themselves, necessarily indicators of national food insecurity. It is the combination of characteristics that is important.

3.2.2 Identifying vulnerable states

It is beyond the scope of this study to provide an all-embracing definition of national food security and a list of all the countries that satisfy it, but some empirical examples are helpful to illustrate the types of country involved and their characteristics. In order to do this, and to focus attention on a manageable number of countries, this report has identified and applied three criteria to indicate states that might be particularly vulnerable to changes in international agricultural trade policy (see Appendix 1). The selec-

tion process is not intended as a definitive measure of vulnerability, but merely as an illustration of the factors to be taken into account and the types of country that might be involved. It has made use of a Commonwealth Secretariat exercise to establish objective indicators of vulnerability.[2]

The need for such criteria arises because there is no operationally effective category in the international trade arena. The NFIDC group is a self-selected assemblage that includes some countries that, while vulnerable to world trade changes (largely by virtue of their small size), would not necessarily be considered particularly food insecure (because of their relative wealth).

The three criteria that have been employed in this study are:

❖ low real GDP *per capita*;

❖ vulnerability;

❖ dependence upon imported food.

For the first criterion, low GDP, we selected the poorest countries in Commonwealth Secretariat/World Bank [1999], Table 2. In addition, we selected from among the next poorest countries those that were also among the most vulnerable as measured by the composite vulnerability index. In other words, we selected the poorest countries and then a group of quite poor and very vulnerable countries. Not all of these countries are highly dependent upon imported food. For the third criterion we used the relative importance of different categories of food imports. Using these criteria, we focused on the 17 States in Tables 5 and 6.

As indicated above, developing countries have been affected in many ways by distorted agricultural markets, and so any change in international agricultural trade policy will have a variety of effects. In order to illustrate this range of effects, we have selected three additional focus states as a reference group. India provides a

---

2 The data for GDP and vulnerability used in this classification were taken from the Commonwealth Secretariat/World Bank Report 'Small States: A Composite Vulnerability Index' [Commonwealth Secretariat/World Bank 1999]. Since then the vulnerability index has been developed further. For a description of the Commonwealth Vulnerability Index see Easter 1999.

contrast, as a very large and poor developing country which is not heavily reliant on food imports but which would be vulnerable to trade regulations that affect its preferred agricultural policies. Egypt represents the very substantial, and quite poor, importing countries that do not feature on our list of vulnerable states (by virtue of being slightly richer) but would nonetheless be affected substantially by trade policy changes that influenced the world market. Argentina illustrates the position of food exporting developing countries.

3.2.3 Characteristics of vulnerable states

One of the principal reasons for focusing in this way on a small, manageable group of states is to observe typical features that can help the reader to understand the ways in which trade policy change may interact with food security policies. The resulting list of 17 states identified through the application of the three criteria is given in Table 5, which provides some basic pieces of information about them.

Table 5 The countries identified as food insecure

Country	Real GDP per capita [a] PPP$	Composite vulnerability index [a]	Population, million [b] 1997 estimate	Agricultural imports as share of total [c] 1994	Imports as share of total cereal supplies [b] 1996
Vulnerable states:					
Congo, Dem. Rep.	300	5.186	48.0	47%	17%
Ethiopia	420	4.786	60.1	21%	4%
São Tomé/Principe	600	7.690	0.1	29%	57%
Myanmar	650	4.392	46.8	33%	0%
Burundi	670	4.929	6.4	20%	15%
Angola	674	6.282	11.6	21%	60%
Malawi	710	5.200	10.1	36%	16%
Rwanda	740	4.797	5.9	27%	61%
Djibouti	775	7.932	0.6	39%	77%
Niger	790	4.957	9.8	30%	4%
Sierra Leone	860	5.060	4.4	62%	51%
Lesotho	980	5.985	2.1	14%	74%
Haiti	1,050	4.474	7.4	82%	59%
Central African Rep.	1,050	4.802	3.4	30%	12%
Gambia	1,190	9.331	1.2	37%	51%
Maldives	2,200	8.654	0.3	16%	108%
Solomon Islands	2,266	8.398	0.4	18%	91%
Reference group:					
India	1,240	3.782	960.2	7%	0%
Egypt	3,800	4.723	64.5	27%	34%
Argentina	8,350	3.539	35.7	6%	1%

Sources: (a) Commonwealth Secretariat/World Bank 1999: Table 2. (b) FAO 1999d. (c) FAO 1996.

Whilst all are quite or very poor (which follows from the selection criteria used), it is clear that they do not form an entirely homogenous group, and nor do they differ unambiguously from the reference states. The two less poor states (both of which have significantly higher real *per capita* GDP than India) have relatively low shares of agricultural goods in total imports. Whilst a high proportion of their cereals is imported, it may be the case that, given their geographical location, cereals are a less important item in diet than is common in Africa or South Asia. Their main justification for inclusion in the list is relatively high vulnerability due, probably, to very small size. By contrast, the main reason for India's exclusion is its very low vulnerability and dependence on international agricultural trade, which relate in part to its very large size.

The difficulty of establishing wholly defensible objective criteria for determining national food insecurity is well illustrated by the case of Egypt. It has a higher dependence on imported cereals than seven of the food insecure states, and has a similar vulnerability index to a further (largely overlapping) group of seven states. The principal reason for its exclusion is its higher *per capita* GDP. But it could well be argued that, at $3,800, it is not so wealthy as to be considered comfortably secure, and with a population of 64.5 million it is likely that there will be large numbers who are both food insecure and heavily dependent for their entitlements on the world market.

Despite these difficulties, the selection serves a purpose in illustrating some features of vulnerable states which, while they are neither common to all nor exclusive, are frequently encountered. Table 6 indicates a number of the characteristics of these states that are relevant to an assessment of the impact of multilateral liberalisation. Most, but not all, of the countries are members of the LLDC group. At the same time, there are many LLDCs that are not in this list because they are not especially dependent on food imports. Hence, while the LLDC category is a useful one in the WTO context, it would be desirable for any special measures in support of food security in developing countries to be made available to a more carefully differentiated group of states which share the characteristics of low income, vulnerability and import dependence.

Many of the countries rely significantly on agriculture for their exports. This means that both sides of their trade-based entitlements are linked to agricultural trade negotiations. Food security could be enhanced or undermined either by changes that affect exports or by those that affect imports.

In most of the countries listed in Table 6, imports supply all or most of the fertiliser consumed. Hence, both trade-related and production entitlements will be affected by international trade policies that affect the price and availability of fertiliser.

Many of those states for which information was available obtain a significant proportion of their total revenue from import taxes. Trade liberalisation will tend to reduce tariff revenue and, hence, require a reorientation of revenue raising. Since trade taxes are important in many developing countries precisely because they are the easiest to collect, it is likely that alternative sources will yield less income. This may have implications for transfer entitlements and for food security policies that aim to enhance production- and trade-related entitlements by government-funded action.

Most of the states are food aid recipients. The figures in the table, which relate to one year (1997), provide only a snapshot and are not an appropriate basis for comparisons between countries. But the table makes the point that, unless 1997 was an unusual year, food aid is a normal part of the food supply equation of such states.

Over half of the countries in the table have recently been involved in a structural adjustment or sectoral adjustment loan from the World Bank. This information is provided as a broad indication as to whether or not substantial domestic liberalisation has been introduced, or is under way. As noted above, some of the changes that might be expected to flow from multilateral liberalisation will not, in fact, occur since the change has already been introduced as a result of structural adjustment.

Table 6 Salient features of focus countries

Countries	LLDC	Agricultural exports as % of total exports[a]	Fertiliser imports as % of consumption[b]	Import taxes as % of total revenue[c]	Cereals food aid as % of total domestic supply[d]	SALs/ SECALs[e]
Vulnerable states:						
Angola	✓	0%	100%	n/a	14%	
Burundi	✓	47%	100%	14%	0%	1992, 1995
Central African Rep.	✓	23%	100%	n/a	2%	
Congo, Dem. Rep.	✓	26%	100%	30%	1%	
Djibouti	✓	22%	n/a	n/a	25%	
Ethiopia	✓	97%	140%	22%	6%	1994, 1995
Gambia	✓	36%	100%	42%	2%	1993
Haiti	✓	25%	100%	n/a	16%	1995
Lesotho	✓	5%	105%	59%	2%	1994
Malawi	✓	80%	100%	n/a	1%	1992, 1993, 1996, 1997
Maldives	✓	0%	n/a	33%	0%	
Myanmar	✓	37%	49%	12%	0%	
Niger	✓	14%	91%	n/a	2%	1994, 1997
Rwanda	✓	29%	100%	25%	28%	1994, 1995
São Tome/Principe	✓	60%	n/a	n/a	1%	
Sierra Leone	✓	15%	100%	49%	5%	1992, 1993, 1994, 1995, 1996, 1997
Solomon Islands	✓	16%	n/a	n/a	0%	
Reference group:						
Argentina	✖	41%	116%	4%		1992, 1993, 1996, 1997, 1998
Egypt	✖	15%	6%	10%	0%	
India	✖	17%	14%	24%		1992

Notes:
(a)   By value, 1996. Source: FAO 1998.
(b)   By volume, 1996. Source: FAO 1999d.
(c)   Latest year available for each country. Source: IMF 1997.
(d)   Cereals food aid from all donors, 1997, as share of total domestic supply of cereals, 1996. Source: FAO 1999d.
(e)   Or other policy-based lending. Source: World Bank Annual Reports, 1992-8.

3.3 Summary of Part 1

This study is rooted in the view that food (in)security is primarily a phenomenon relating to individuals, and is determined by three sets of factors concerned with supply, access and guarantees to food. In the multilateral world, by contrast, food security is considered as a state affair, and discussion tends to focus on adequate supplies of imported food. The study has used the entitlements approach to assessing individual food security both to identify the ways in which international trade might impinge (as well as the other non-trade-related factors at work) and, by analogy, to identify the characteristics that would tend to make some countries more food insecure than others.

Food security may be said to be determined by:

❖ production-based entitlements, which will be influenced by policies that affect the demand and supply of factors affecting production, some of which will relate to international trade;

❖ trade-based entitlements, which will be influenced by policies that affect the level and variability of food prices in relation to the price of what individuals are able to exchange for food; in cases where there are substantial agricultural exports, trade-based entitlements are likely to be affected by policy on both sides of the trade balance;

❖ labour-based entitlements, which are influenced by the level and location of employment opportunities which may, in turn, be influenced by trade policy;

❖ transfer-based entitlements, which

include formal transfers from governments and aid donors that may be influenced by multilateral trade agreements.

By analogy, the food security of a state can be said to depend upon:

❖ its production entitlements, which reflect the food that can be produced domestically;

❖ its trade entitlements, which reflect its ability to earn sufficient foreign exchange with exports to purchase imported food; and

❖ its transfer entitlements, which cover food that can be obtained either directly through food aid or indirectly by (semi-) commercial imports financed through financial aid.

Food insecure states are those where both production and trade entitlements are problematic: the country's agricultural production is insufficient or too irregular to guarantee adequate supplies every year, and export revenue is not sufficiently strong to give confidence that, regardless of the state of the world market, food could be imported to make up any shortfall without severe consequences for other import-dependent areas. (It may be assumed that any state that is dependent upon transfer entitlements for an adequate supply is food insecure, since aid is intrinsically unreliable in the medium term.)

In order to illustrate some common characteristics of food insecure states, three criteria have been derived from this analysis. They relate to GDP, vulnerability and dependence on imported food. A group of 17 states has been compiled, together with a reference group of three others. Between them, they exemplify the differing interests of developing countries in international agricultural trade.

Part 2

Policies
Chapter 4: Entitlement Promotion and Protection Policies

Part 1 described some of the many ways in which production, trade, labour and transfer entitlements are obtained. It provides a foundation for the review in this chapter of the main *policies* that have been used to enhance such entitlements.

While almost all government policies will affect entitlements, directly or indirectly, concern for food security has given rise to a number of policies which aim directly to improve it. These can be subdivided into:

❖ *entitlement promotion policies*, which aim to increase the overall level of individual or household entitlements; and

❖ *entitlement protection policies*, which aim to prevent individual/household entitlements from falling below a certain level.

An important subset of entitlement promotion policies are those which aim to increase individual or household production over time. These include research and extension (R+E) services, measures to encourage more intensive use of chemical and organic inputs such as fertiliser subsidies, the introduction of higher-yielding crop varieties, and investment subsidies. Also important are policies towards marketing. Important entitlement protection policies are food price subsidies, food stamps, targeted feeding programmes and labour-intensive public works.

For the sake of clarity, such food security policies have been grouped into five categories: food production, marketing, labour, transfers and safety nets, and enabling macro and sectoral policies. The first four will impact primarily upon production, trade, labour and transfer en-titlements respectively. It is important to keep in mind, however, that some policies span more than one group, and that each policy is likely to have indirect effects on other forms of entitlement.

Table 7 lists the most important food security policies, in order of relevance to developing countries. Relevance has been determined on the basis of effectiveness, cost and political and administrative feasibility.

4.1 Food Production

Increasing the food output of smallholder farmers by definition enhances their production-based entitlements. It will also, *ceteris paribus*, lower food prices and thus improve trade-based enti-tlements for net food consumers [Sijm 1997]. The resulting increased income can also reduce household vulnerability to short-term reductions in entitlements if it is used to reinforce the asset base of the poor [IFPRI 1992].

Increased food production will also affect other groups. For example, it can often increase the demand for hired labour, boosting the labour-based entitlements of landless labourers [IFPRI 1992]. Those relying on non-agricultural employment for labour-based entitlements may also benefit, as a result of increased demand for local goods and services [Mellor 1986; Hazell and Roell 1983].

There are, however, some caveats that must be added to this positive picture. Production-increasing policies which raise capital intensity may reduce, rather than enhance, the demand for labourers on farms [IFPRI 1992]. Likewise, production-increasing policies must ensure that they reach the poorest farmers, who otherwise can suffer from higher rents and input prices.

Table 7 Food security policies and entitlements

Policy by category	Policy
Food production (production entitlements)	1 Input credit 2 Subsidised or free inputs 3 Research and extension 4 Capital expenditure and investment promotion 5 Land reform
Marketing (trade entitlements)	1 Market development and regulation 2 Parastatal reform 3 Food price stabilisation (buffer stocks) 4 Food price stabilisation (buffer funds)
Labour (labour entitlements)	1 High-value export crops 2 Small- and medium-enterprise development 3 Micro-finance 4 Minimum wages
Transfers and safety nets (transfer entitlements)	1 Labour-intensive public works programmes 2 Targeted feeding programmes 3 Food stamps 4 Food price subsidies
Enabling macro and sectoral policies	1 Infrastructure (transport, communications) 2 Exchange rate policy 3 Health 4 Education

Production-increasing policies can be divided broadly into:

❖ measures to provide recurrent support to farmers (such as credit and support to encourage the more intensive use of inputs such as fertiliser);

❖ R+E services; and

❖ capital expenditure and investment promotion.

4.1.1 Input credit

Input credit can contribute to food production by relieving the cash constraints of poorer households, thus enabling them to purchase production-increasing inputs [Sijm 1997; Pinstrup-Anderson 1989; Amin 1990]. Imperfections in financial markets often mean that, in the absence of government interventions, input credit will not be available for poorer households even though smaller producers often rely more on credit than larger producers. Improving access to credit is likely to benefit smaller producers disproportionately [Mukherjee 1994].

Such credit may be made available to poorer households through a number of different institutions, such as state banks, integrated rural development agencies, commercial banks, lending groups or co-operatives. Credit can be made more available to poorer households/individuals by subsidising interest rates, regulating loans made by public and private institutions or linking credit to the delivery of other services such as input delivery [Sijm 1997].

4.1.2 Input subsidies

Governments have also taken measures to encourage the more intensive use of chemical and organic inputs, in particular by subsidising fertiliser. These have helped to increase the production of food, in particular among smaller farmers for whom lack of inputs and lack of money to purchase inputs is often a key constraint to increasing production [Drèze and Sen 1989]. The provision of input subsidies has also assisted smaller farmers to benefit from other policy changes, such as devaluations for exporting farmers and reduced taxation of agriculture [Woodward 1995].

Fertiliser subsidies have become less common following structural adjustment, which has led, either directly or indirectly (by reducing government budgets), to a reduction in expenditure on such subsidies. They are not now widely used in adjusting countries. On the other hand, targeted distribution of fertilisers and seeds is increasingly popular, delivered either free of charge to food deficit smallholders or through self-targeted labour-intensive 'inputs-for-work' programmes.

4.1.3 Research and extension services

There is broad agreement in the literature on the importance of R+E services in improving agricultural practice, in facilitating the development and introduction of new technologies in the agricultural sector, and in enabling smaller farmers to take advantage of other policies such as devaluation [Woodward 1995]. But there is less agreement as to the form this should take.

Since the Green Revolution in Asia, the training and visit (T+V) extension approach has been promoted by international research centres, aid agencies and national governments alike [Scoones 1998b]. In the T+V, or Transfer of Technology, paradigm, 'research decisions are made by scientists and technology is developed on research stations, and then handed to extension to pass on to others' [Pretty and Chambers 1994]. It has resulted in some successes. One example is the development of higher-yielding crops, location-specific fertiliser recommendations and improved farming practices in Malawi [Sijm 1997].

However, T+V has also been widely criticised. Critics have focused on its supply-driven nature. They argue that it is prescriptive and pays insufficient attention to local conditions [Scoones 1998b; Pretty and Chambers 1994]. Performance of agricultural research stations, such as the Department of Agricultural Research in Malawi, has also been seen to be low in relation to the resources they receive [Sijm 1997].

These critics support an alternative, 'farmer-first' perspective in which R+E centres around the knowledge and practices of farmers themselves. They see the role of R+E as to facilitate farmers in undertaking their own experimentation, to encourage the sharing of new technologies, to assist group inquiry and experimentation, and to accept context specificity and the complexity of the world and individual situations (see Box 1). The farmer-first approach does acknowledge the need for formal research to be carried out within research stations, but implies that those carrying out research must also learn from and listen to farmers [Pretty and Chambers 1994].

Box 1 The Soil and Water Conservation Branch, Kenya

Kenya's soil and water conservation branch provides an example of a 'farmer-first' research and extension system which has been successful in increasing agricultural yields, and promoting environmental and economic regeneration and resource conservation without requiring direct subsidisation.

In 1987, after the failure of the existing 'traditional' R+E system to support sufficient soil and water conservation measures, the ministry of agriculture adopted a 'catchment' approach. Teams of extension officers from different ministries worked for a specific period of time in each 'catchment' area. They used participatory rural appraisal (PRA) techniques to analyse the social and ecological conditions giving rise to soil erosion, produce inventories of local knowledge and practices, and develop action plans. These plans were then discussed at an open meeting to which farmers were invited. Action plans were discussed and farmers given the opportunity to comment. A catchment committee, comprised of local people, with responsibility for co-ordinating water and soil conservation was then elected.

Sources: MALDM 1988 – 93; Pretty et al. 1994.

These two perspectives are not mutually exclusive. The T+V system has worked well in areas in which there are relatively simple technological packages and in which conditions are relatively homogenous. The farmer-first perspective, by contrast, is more successful in complex, diverse and risk-prone areas.

4.1.4 Capital expenditure

Capital expenditure, for example on irrigation, can help to increase and stabilise food production by allowing higher and more stable yields. Irrigation can also help to encourage higher-yielding production methods such as double cropping, reduce the risks involved in adopting new technologies and may also expand the land available for cultivation.

Irrigation can be provided by either public or private agents, or some combination of both. Large-scale, purely public projects do not have a very successful track record, suffering from high costs of investment and maintenance, poor management and corruption. However, complete privatisation is also likely to have adverse effects on food security because poorer farmers are likely to be excluded. Privatisation can also result in high transactions costs. The most desirable form of provision, therefore, appears to be a combination of public and private, such as can be achieved by more participatory forms of irrigation management or the separation of capital costs and maintenance [Sijm 1997].

Governments can also provide subsidies for investment, in order to encourage farmers to improve technologies, purchase productive assets or new inputs, or increase land holdings. This can be an important way of increasing production for those farmers which are deterred from undertaking investments, for example due to a lack of access to credit. But it remains an area of controversy.

4.1.5 Land reform

Lack of land is often a critical constraint to production for smallholder producers [Christensen and Stack 1992]. In such circumstances, land reform has the potential to increase production substantially. Land reform may also increase the benefits that smallholders can obtain from adjustment programmes, for example in Malawi [Cromwell 1992; Woodward 1995]. However it is extremely difficult politically, and is therefore less effective as a food security policy, particularly in the short run.

4.2 Marketing
4.2.1 Market development and regulation

There is widespread agreement in the literature that a minimum requirement of government is to provide the regulatory framework and information to allow private markets to function effectively [Baulch 1999; Abbott 1987]. Particularly important in a context of increasing private sector involvement in food marketing is the development of 'agricultural marketing information systems' (AMIS) and the dissemination of this information through local media, for the benefit not only of traders but also producers and consumers.

4.2.2 Parastatal reform

In the pre-structural adjustment era, parastatal marketing boards had the sole, or primary, responsibility in many countries for the marketing of output, defined as 'business activities associated with the flow of goods and services from production to consumption' [Abbott 1987: 1]. This resulted in well documented problems of inefficiency, political appointments and corruption. These factors increased costs, which widened margins between producer and consumer costs, reducing the trade-based entitlements of both groups. In addition, many state marketing boards required subsidisation, with associated budgetary costs [Baulch 1999]. In some cases, it has even been argued that state marketing boards contributed directly to food insecurity by failing to move grain into deficit areas [see Box 2, and also Rukuni and Jayne 1995 and Christensen and Stack 1992 on Zimbabwe].

The worst excesses of such marketing boards have been phased out by and large by SAPs and, while the problems of state marketing boards are widely known, there remains some debate as to the proper role of the state in food marketing [Baulch 1999]. Some argue that the state should provide only infrastructure and public goods. Others feel that there remains a role for parastatals in promoting food security. Private traders may not serve areas in which marketed surpluses are low – often precisely the areas in which the poorer farmers are located. In Malawi, for example, privatisation of ADMARC resulted in large gaps in the marketing network following the closure of all points in which less than 60 tonnes of grain per year were purchased. Overcoming this problem has required a continued role for ADMARC, which has filled the gap by transporting inputs to and grain away from these areas in order to protect trade entitlements [Cromwell 1992].

4.2.3 Price stabilisation (buffer stocks)

Parastatals may also have a role in maintaining buffer stocks in order to preserve food for emergencies and stabilise prices (see Box 3). Given the dependence of domestic food production on the weather, the seasonal nature of production and the inelastic nature of supply, price variability can be large in many countries. Such instability can have negative effects on both producers and consumers, and increase the variability of their trade-based entitlements. This is a particular problem for poorer consumers, for whom food represents a higher proportion of income than other groups [Baulch 1999]. Price volatility can also serve to discourage investment [IFPRI 1992; Pinckney 1993]. It also increases transactions costs, in particular for small producers [Pinckney 1993].

One proposed avenue for government policies to limit price instability is the creation of a stockpile of the staple produce. By purchasing in good years and selling in bad years, it may be possible to maintain prices within a specified band [Baulch 1999]. The degree to which this can be done successfully will depend upon country-specific factors, such as the degree to which production fluctuates, location and infrastructure [IFPRI 1992].

Even when country-specific factors are favourable, there are costs and difficulties with maintaining buffer stocks. First, as Baulch [1999] points out, it is often difficult to know whether a particular year is a 'good' year or a 'bad' year. Second, the costs of public storage can be very high, particularly in comparison with private sector storage. In addition to the budgetary cost, there is also the opportunity cost of using resources in order to maintain buffer stocks rather than for other food security policies [Baulch 1999; IFPRI 1992].

As a result of such cost considerations, there is now increasing recognition that a 'minimalist' approach to price stabilisation may be the most appropriate. That is, government action should be to keep prices within a fairly wide band, and merely 'lean into the wind' [Baulch 1999; IFPRI 1992; Pinckney 1993].

4.2.4 Price stabilisation (buffer funds)

A further policy option, which may involve lower costs than domestic storage, is to make up food shortfalls by importing using the foreign currency earned by exporting in good years [Baulch 1999]. The efficacy of such a strategy depends on the degree to which production fluctuations are correlated between the country and the rest of the world (particularly in major trading partners) and on the reliability of transport systems. There may also be political reasons for governments not to want to rely on international trade in order to meet their food needs. However, the maintenance of buffer funds may enable governments to stabilise prices at a lower

cost than that of maintaining a physical stock of food [Baulch 1999].

4.3 Labour

The entitlements approach makes it clear that food security depends on incomes as much as on trade or food production. Incomes will be affected by a range of policy and non-policy factors, not all of which can be described here. However, four policies (not necessarily focused on agriculture) are of particular relevance to the promotion of labour entitlements: high-value export crops, small and medium enterprise (SME) development, micro-finance and minimum wages.

4.3.1 High-value export crops

High-value export crops can provide labour entitlements to individuals and households both directly (smallholders producing for export) or, more commonly, through employment on exporting farms [Cromwell 1992]. There is a general consensus that such crops need to be balanced with the production of food for household consumption [Maxwell 1999; IFPRI 1992]. Poorer households, which tend to be more risk averse, will often continue production of food crops primarily for domestic consumption even while there are significant incentives for them to engage in export production. Structural adjustment programmes have aimed typically to increase the incentives for high-value export crop production, in particular through devaluation. However, there is now increasing recognition that additional policy measures (such as those described in other parts of this chapter) are required to enable smaller farmers to respond to such incentives [Cromwell 1992; Maxwell 1999].

Gender issues may also be involved with the promotion of marketed crops if these are seen as 'men's crops' and the incomes obtained are therefore under the control of men. This means that they may not increase the food security of women and children as much as increased incomes that are under female control.

4.3.2 SME development

Even in rural areas, labour-based entitlements need not relate directly to agriculture. Over the past decade, the role of SMEs (often in manufacturing) in providing employment and thus increasing labour entitlements has been recognised increasingly. SMEs are particularly important too in that it is often women that are employed by small-scale entrepreneurs. If high-value marketed crops are affected by gender bias, increased labour entitlements from SMEs may feed through more directly into increased food security for women and children [Pinstrup-Anderson 1989]. SMEs can also be important in promoting the entitlements of other groups: small-scale traders, for example, may increase the trade entitlements of small farmers [Green 1994].

The need for public support for SMEs is also widely recognised. SMEs, in particular in rural areas, can suffer from a lack of access to credit, technologies and business management skills. To help them to overcome these problems, most developing countries have some sort of SME support agency which provides a range of services to SMEs [see, for example, Ratnam 1991 on India; IBRD 1994 on Malaysia; ITC 1997 on Bangladesh]. The importance of providing these services collectively and encouraging inter-firm co-operation is also being increasingly highlighted in the literature [see, for example, Humphrey and Schmitz 1996].

4.3.3 Micro-finance

One example of support to small entrepreneurs that has met with particular success in developing countries has been micro-finance, in which very small loans are made to micro-entrepreneurs. The most well-known example of such a scheme is the Grameen Bank in Bangladesh. Following its example, micro-credit schemes are being developed in many other developing countries. The small size of the loans and the use of group lending instead of collateral has meant that repayment rates are often extremely high. The schemes are therefore highly cost effective.

4.3.4 Minimum wage legislation

Minimum wage legislation can also increase incomes and thus promote the labour entitlements of poorer individuals and households. However, such legislation, by increasing wages, may also increase unemployment. The overall effects will therefore depend on the structure of labour markets and the relative bargaining power of workers *vis-à-vis* employers. Minimum wage legislation may also be less effective in reaching the poorest households or individuals, who often rely on informal or temporary employment and for whom such legislation may not apply. This suggests that it is a less effective means of increasing the labour-based entitlements than other policies described above.

4.4 Transfers and Safety Nets

Since the 1990 *World Development Report* [IBRD 1990], transfers and safety nets have been seen as essential for entitlement protection and promotion. The former involves the transfer of resources to poorer households or individuals: the aim is redistributive. Safety nets, by contrast, aim to provide insurance to vulnerable groups, who may experience a deterioration in their entitlements at particular times.

An important issue in the literature on transfers and safety nets is around targeting, defined as the identification and selection of certain areas, groups, households or individuals for the receipt of particular benefits [Besley and Kanbur 1993]. Non-targeted transfers include generalised food subsidies. Targeted ones include food stamps or labour-intensive public works. Given the budgetary constraints in most developing countries, there is a general agreement that targeting is now necessary in order to protect and promote entitlements in the most cost effective way [IBRD 1990].

There is less agreement on the most useful method of targeting. It can be done by the individual or groups themselves ('self-targeting'), by administrators ('administrative targeting') or by communities ('community targeting'). Within administrative targeting, too, there are different mechanisms: direct means-testing is one option, but this is expensive and difficult particularly in a developing country context [IBRD 1990]. Administrative targeting has therefore focused on the use of indicators that can be used as proxies – characteristics of groups (sex,age, region, nutritional status) which tend to be correlated with food insecurity [IBRD 1990].

4.4.1 Labour-intensive public works

For households with at least one able-bodied member, labour-intensive public works programmes are widely agreed to be a successful and cost effective means of increasing labour-based entitlements (see Box 4). Such programmes provide either food or cash in return for work on public projects, often involving the provision of infrastructure. Such projects rely on self-targeting: only those really at risk of being food insecure are likely to take part, in particular if wages provided are slightly below the market wage [Gaiha 1993]. By providing guaranteed incomes, they can prevent distress sales of household assets which can have long-term implications for poverty alleviation [van der Walle 1995]. They can also result in the creation of assets that encourage longer-term increases in production and trade-based entitlements [Devereux 1999]. Although there are some costs to such programmes, such as the forgone labour of the poor [Ravallion and Datt 1995], this problem can largely be overcome if such works are integrated with the seasonal work patterns of the poor [Green 1994].

Box 4 Employment guarantee scheme in Maharashtra, India

Possibly the most well-known example of a labour intensive public works, Maharashtra's Employment Guarantee Scheme (EGS) was first introduced in 1970 and has since expanded so that attendance has been around 100 million person-days in recent years. During the 1972 – 3 drought in Maharashtra, in some villages wages from public works were more than 50% of total incomes. The scheme provides unskilled manual labour on demand on small-scale, rural public works projects such as roads, irrigation facilities and reforestation.

Available data suggest that the scheme is well-targeted, with a clearly negative correlation between consumption expenditure and participation in the scheme. Self-targeting, in the form of less desirable work (basic agricultural labour) and low wages, was clearly effective.

It has been estimated that one-quarter of income gained from the EGS displaces income from other sources, with a higher figure for men than for women. However, they did not consider other costs associated with the scheme, such as administration, supervision and other non-wage costs.

In general, however, Maharashtra's EGS has been very effective in increasing the entitlements of the poor in the most cost-effective manner.

Sources: Ravallion and Datt 1995; Drèze and Sen 1989.

4.4.2 Targeted feeding programmes

Targeted feeding programmes provide food directly to vulnerable groups, which can be identified geographically, by means testing, by age (e.g. feeding programmes) or by vulnerability assessments (see Box 5). Their advantages are that they can increase food consumption more than giving cash directly, given that the income elasticity of food expenditure is normally less than one [IFPRI 1992]. As with food stamps, they can also offer additional benefits such as encouraging children to attend school [IFPRI 1992]. Providing food to vulnerable groups in times of distress can also encourage them to produce more and to conserve their assets, thus increasing overall livelihood security for such groups [Green 1994].

Such programmes can also be costly, with high administrative demands [IFPRI 1992]. They are therefore most appropriate when other mechanisms for increasing entitlements, such as labour-intensive public works, are not appropriate (for example, because the target group is not able-bodied).

Box 5 Targeted feeding in Tamil Nadu, India

Tamil Nadu's noonday meals scheme was started in 1982, and provided free school meals and feeding for infants. It has since been extended to cover old-age pensioners, ex-servicemen and widows living below the poverty line.

In a study of North Arcot, Tamil Nadu, Harriss [1992] found that take-up of meals was almost universal, and that, in a comparison of a higher- and lower-income village F and E errors were higher in the richer and poorer villages respectively. One concern, however, is that as 60% of school dropouts are female, boys may receive more than girls.

As with other such schemes, feeding in Tamil Nadu is costly, at 10% of the state budget. This is financed out of general revenue, additional taxes on luxuries, voluntary contributions and compulsory contributions out of government salaries.

Source: Cornia and Stewart 1995.

Box 6 Food stamps in Sri Lanka

In 1977, the universal rice, wheat and sugar subsidy that had previously been in place in Sri Lanka was reduced and then replaced by targeted food stamps. These were issued to households on the basis of income and the number of children. Stamps were issued for a fixed nominal sum. This was not increased in line with inflation and therefore fell in real terms: by 1981 – 2 the real value of the stamps was less than half that of the value of the rice rations previously in place.

The shift to a food stamp scheme resulted in a large increased in F-mistakes: 29% of the bottom quintile of the population did not receive food stamps. As a result, the nutritional standard of the bottom 20% of the population worsened considerably. Part of the reason for the fall in value of the food stamps over time was the significant loss of political support as the transfer moved from a general to a targeted one.

Sources: Cornia and Stewart 1995; IBRD 1990.

4.4.3 Food stamps

Food stamps are a targeted transfer given to particular groups. They give such groups a quota, measured in nominal currency, to enable them to purchase food [IBRD 1990]. Distribution of food stamps is often done through other public services such as health clinics [Devereux 1999].

Given their targeted nature, food stamps can be much more successful than generalised food subsidies in raising the trade-based entitlements of the poor in a cost effective manner (Box 6). Distribution through clinics or other public services can increase the use of such services [Devereux 1999] and reduce the costs of the exercise [IFPRI 1992]. Food stamps can also increase the proportion of income that is spent on food [IFPRI 1992].

There are also disadvantages. Most importantly, food stamps fail to protect consumers against short-term price fluctuations for food [IFPRI 1992]. Distribution of the stamps may fail to reach the poorest households [Cornia and Stewart 1995]. They may also be infeasible politically [Devereux 1999]. Generally, therefore, food stamps are less successful than targeted feeding and labour-intensive public works as a means of increasing the entitlements of the poor.

4.4.4 Food price subsidies

Food price subsidies reduce the cost of food for consumers, thereby increasing their trade-based entitlements (Box 7). They can also have substitution effects, as food becomes cheaper relative to other goods, thereby increasing consumption

[Devereux, 1999]. Most such subsidies have been general – that is, available on all food.

Box 7 General food price subsidies in Egypt

Egypt has had a food subsidy system comprised of an unrestricted subsidy on coarse/refined flour and bread, with ration cards for other basic commodities. Unlike many countries, Egypt does have rural ration shops, meaning that rural consumers have almost as much access as urban consumers to subsidised food.

As a result of the subsidies, Egypt has had higher levels of nutrition than would be expected for its income level. It has been estimated, for example, that the subsidies have resulted in an increased calorie consumption of 100 – 200 per day in poorer households [Alderman and von Braun 1984]. The good rural coverage has also resulted in low F-mistakes.

However, E-mistakes have been high and as a result the scheme is very costly: of 10 – 15% of total government expenditure during the 1970s and 1980s. This has resulted in large budget deficits in Egypt, and has placed it under pressure to reform the scheme.

Source: Cornia and Stewart 1995.

General food price subsidies have a number of advantages as a mechanism for improving trade-based entitlements. First, they are administratively simple and have very low administrative costs [Devereux 1999]. They are also politically feasible, as powerful groups also benefit substantially from them [Devereux 1999]. They have been useful in encouraging private traders to move food into areas in which there are shortages, for example during droughts in India [IFPRI 1992].

Against these merits, generalised food subsidies have substantial costs. They have been phased out in many developing countries, in particular during SAPs. Most importantly, they are extremely costly in financial terms [Devereux 1999; Pinstrup-Anderson 1989]. They can also result in very low levels of subsidy per poor person due to overall financial cost constraints. This makes them relatively ineffective at improving entitlements [Cornia and Stewart 1995]. Moreover, subsidised food may not even be available to certain segments of the food insecure populations, such as those located in rural areas [Devereux 1999]. Given that total food consumption is likely to be higher in richer households, too, their overall effect is regressive [IFPRI 1992]. In sum, therefore, generalised food subsidies are an ineffective way of improving the entitlements of the poor.

Chapter 5: Trade Policies

Chapter 4 illustrates that food security *policies* encompass a wide range of actions, many of which might be affected directly or indirectly by trade liberalisation. The ways in which agricultural trade has been distorted in the past, and may well be liberalised in the future, have been explained in Chapter 3. The present section links these two sets of information. It reviews analytically the types of effect that could be produced on the sources of entitlements noted above by different types of liberalisation. It then relates this information to a consideration of the WTO agenda.

5.1 The Relationship Between Trade Policy and Food Security

5.1.1 Types of effect

Absolute and relative
Changes in trade-related policy are likely to have relative effects, and these may be more important for food security than the absolute change. These relative effects will principally be between:

- ❖ tradables and non-tradables;

- ❖ sectors (those in which policy has changed most *vis-à-vis* the others);

- ❖ products within sectors (for example, between agricultural products that are for export, for domestic consumption but compete with imports, or for domestic consumption and don't compete).

Because of these relative product changes, there will also be relative geographical and social changes. Some social-gender groups will be affected more than others (positively or negatively) if they are more associated with one group

of products than the others. There will be similar differential effects on geographical regions (both within and between countries).

Past and future
Much of the change resulting from SAPs has happened already. States may, or may not, keep 'taking the medicine', but the big shock from a closed to an open economy will have happened, and evidence should be feeding through. This is not the case with the Uruguay Round. Many of the changes agreed in the Round were modest – but there is probably more to come. It is important, therefore, to identify the types of effect that may not have happened yet but which could be on the cards if the WTO continues along its current path.

Domestic and foreign
An individual's/social group's food security will be affected both by what their national government does and by the consequences of changes by other countries. As a rule of thumb, one can argue that the impact of SAPs on food security is most evident in changes to domestic policy, but (especially for SSA) the impact of the Uruguay Round will be felt mainly through the actions of other countries.

The principal changes that have occurred to domestic trade-related policies that might affect food security are those involved with: liberalisation of international trade policy, changes to macroeconomic policies with external consequences, and changes to policies on agricultural development. At the same time, both the import- and export-related determinants of food security noted above may be affected by the trade policy changes of other countries.

5.1.2 Effects of domestic liberalisation

Trade policy

Both SAPs and the Uruguay Round have involved tariffication and a general reduction in tariff levels. But while SAPs may well have had an impact on food security (by reducing trade barriers and hence making imported food cheaper relative to domestic production), as explained below, it is unlikely that the tariff provisions of the Uruguay Round have had any significant effect in this way. The next WTO negotiations might do so (or, at least, reduce the possibility of reversing SAP changes).

Macroeconomic policy

The most important macroeconomic policy for the international dimension of food security is the exchange rate. This is exclusively a SAP matter: there is no WTO provision on exchange rates. Countries that have introduced effective devaluations (i.e. a change in the nominal exchange rate that is not offset by subsequent inflation) will have altered the relative price of internationally traded goods and domestically traded/non-traded products. Since this will affect all traded goods, it should not have differential product effects. But it will tend to have favoured producers over consumers (and, hence, will have differential social effects).

Agricultural subsidies

The issue most likely to link SAPs/WTO and agricultural development is that of subsidies to agriculture. Either as a result of deliberate policy or simply as a consequence of reduced government expenditure, SAPs have often resulted in lower government subsidies to agriculture. The Uruguay Round also has provisions on subsidies. While, as explained below, it is unlikely that these will bite in any country in SSA, the next Round of multilateral trade negotiations could impinge more strongly on developing country freedom of manoeuvre.

5.1.3 Effects of international liberalisation

To the extent that the Uruguay Round has had an effect on food security, it is more likely to have been mediated through changes in policy by other countries. Broadly speaking, these will have affected the agricultural products that developing countries import, those that they export, and world price stability.

Effects on imports

The food security of some vulnerable groups will almost certainly have been affected in the past by Northern agricultural subsidies. These have depressed the world price of various temperate agricultural goods, of which cereals are probably the most important. In a static sense, this has made it easier to supply food-deficit countries with imported cereals. Whether this static 'gain' has been offset by a dynamic 'loss' (because it has dulled incentives for domestic agricultural growth) is a moot point. But, to the extent that they exist, both static and dynamic effects will change if Northern agriculture is liberalised. The initial effect is expected to be an increase in world prices, especially for cereals.

Effects on exports

Multilateral liberalisation will affect the price of some developing country exports, but the impact will vary considerably according to the product and the market. The broad effect is that a reduction of import tariffs by developed countries should increase their demand for imports, including those from developing countries. But how this affects particular developing countries, and therefore food security, depends both upon the current trade regime for the products they export and their capacity to alter supply in response to increased demand.

Paradoxically, many SSA exports will not benefit initially from liberalisation and, indeed, may suffer. This is partly because traditional agricultural exports (such as beverages) already face very low tariffs worldwide and so will be unaffected one way or the other. In addition, those agricultural exports that do face heavy protectionism (such as sugar, tobacco and horticulture) have preferential access to the European market, which absorbs the great bulk of exports. To the extent that the EU liberalises, it will adversely affect SSA exporters either by increasing competition from less favoured suppliers or by reducing prices in the protected European market. This reasoning does not apply, however, to South Asia or to parts of Latin America (such as Mercosur), which receive no such preferences in the EU. Moreover, if SSA states could increase their output sufficiently to take advantage of liberalisation in non-EU industrialised country markets (as, for example, the Andean countries – which also receive deep preferences – have done) where the Uruguay Round and its successors will genuinely improve their access, then they, too, could benefit.

Effects on price volatility

We could expect an increase in world price volatility to affect adversely food security on the assumption that the vulnerable are less able to deal with shocks. Unfortunately, it is very difficult to say what effect global liberalisation will have, at least in the short to medium term, on price instability. In principle, full liberalisation should reduce instability (by increasing the number of producers and consumers who adjust to supply shocks). But the world's progress towards liberalisation will be very crab-like. In the short term it may well be the case that changes likely to increase volatility will exceed those likely to reduce it.

This is because Northern policy changes that reduce the size of stockpiles are likely to come on stream before those that open up markets. By reducing publicly held stocks, the world's capacity to supply food insecure countries with subsidised exports or food aid is reduced. The opening up of markets would tend to operate in the opposite direction, by giving incentives to a larger number of countries to increase their production (thus reducing the world's reliance on a small number of sources). But it is unlikely that there will be sufficient liberalisation in the short to medium term to justify any substantial increases in production among, for example, the Cairns Group countries.

5.2 The Link With the WTO Agenda

5.2.1 Food security and multilateral trade policies

Not all of the policies described in Chapter 4 will be affected by every, or even necessarily any, item likely to be on the agenda of the next Round of multilateral agricultural trade liberalisation. But most will be potentially affected to some extent. The relationship is sketched in Table 8, which extends the analytical framework established in Table 7. The right-hand column provides a broad-brush indication of the ways in which each of the food security policies identified in Chapter 4 might be affected by changes to multilateral trade agreements.

In cases where a policy depends upon government expenditure the reduction of tariffs is likely to have an impact, at least during an adjustment period (which could be quite lengthy) before the introduction of alternative sources of government revenue. In addition, policies that require government to spend directly in the agricultural sector could be affected by future changes both on the allowable areas of domestic subsidy and on the total permitted volume of subsidy. Those policies that involve providing the vulnerable with subsidised food will often be supported by concessional imports. These may be affected in turn by the outcome of the next round of negotiations on export subsidies (particularly if this goes beyond dealing with direct subsidies to cover cross-subsidy from the protected domestic market).

Table 8 Food security policies and international trade policy

Policy by category	Policy	Potentially affected by trade policy on:
Food production (production entitlements)	1 Input credit 2 Subsidised or free inputs 3 Research and extension 4 Capital expenditure and investment promotion 5 Land reform	Domestic subsidies Domestic subsidies Tariffs (revenue) Domestic subsidies –
Marketing (trade entitlements)	1 Market development and regulation 2 Parastatal reform 3 Food price stabilisation (buffer stocks) 4 Food price stabilisation (buffer funds)	– State trading enterprises Domestic subsidies (including Green Box conditions on buffer stocks/funds) Export regulation Tariffs, Green Box conditions on buffer stocks/funds
Labour (labour entitlements)	1 High-value export crops 2 Small- and medium-enterprise development 3 Micro-finance 4 Minimum wages	Developed country market access Domestic subsidies – – Process criteria
Transfers and safety nets (transfer entitlements)	1 Labour-intensive public works programmes 2 Targeted feeding programmes 3 Food stamps 4 Food price subsidies	Export subsidies Export subsidies Export subsidies Domestic subsidies

As is clear from Chapter 4, not all of these food security policies are widely accepted as desirable, and even some that are supported in principle are not feasible financially or politically. The broad order of feasibility/desirability is indicated in the table by the order in which they are presented within each cell. The policy numbered (1) has the highest priority.

5.2.2 Preserving food security policies

It is clear from Part 1 and the preceding sub-section that the existing distortions of world agricultural trade have had profound effects on global supply and demand, so that liberalisation is likely to affect the food security status of many people and groups. In addition, the ways in which new trade rules are framed may alter the feasibility of the policies currently employed or recommended to promote or protect individual food security. The summary information in Table 8 suggests that the key food security policy concerns in the next agricultural trade Round are:

❖ Ensuring that tariff cuts do not occur in such a manner as to reduce government revenue required for recurrent and capital support to domestic production (especially for small farmers), and the provision of transfers and safety nets (which largely means ensuring that there is an adequate transition period and appropriate technical and capital assistance to enable alternative sources of government revenue to be obtained).

❖ Ensuring that the regime on domestic agricultural subsidies is framed in such a way as to avoid undermining agricultural development policies that involve government support that is production-related (and needs to be so if it is to bolster food security, e.g. because it aims to increase either the production or trade entitlements of poor farmers). At present, expenditure on agriculture is often lower than is desirable and the availability of finance is likely to remain a key constraint on any increase. But it is important to avoid a situation in which (whether by accident or design) additional hurdles are put in place that make it even harder to provide the agricultural sector with the recurrent and investment support that it requires.

❖ Ensuring that if policies on subsidised exports are tightened substantially adjustment measures are put in place (through the provision of either food or financial aid) to enable countries that have food-based safety nets to continue to operate them until alternative, equally effective, food security policies have been established.

5.3 Summary of Part 2

Government policy is only one influence on the entitlements identified in Part 1, and the subset described specifically as 'food security policies' represents only one part of the picture. They are, nonetheless, important. Part 2 has shown how the entitlements identified in Part 1 can be promoted or protected by various government interventions, and it has reviewed the evidence on the desirability and feasibility of such policies.

This analysis demonstrates the breadth of policies that can have a direct impact on food security. They include measures to promote food production, facilitate the operations of markets, enhance the availability and value of labour entitlements, and provide transfers and safety nets. In addition, enabling macro and sectoral policies will have an indirect effect on food security.

Multilateral trade negotiations may affect this pattern of government action in two ways:

❖ by introducing change to the policies (of both domestic and foreign governments) that impact directly on entitlements (for example, by altering the food prices paid by consumers or received by producers);

❖ by making more or less feasible some of the policies that are considered desirable to promote or protect entitlements.

For each of the major policies identified in Chapter 5, Chapter 6 draws a link to the multilateral arena to determine whether, and by what means, they could be affected by any change to international trade rules. It demonstrates that most of the policies could be affected. The multilateral policy areas most likely to affect entitlement protection and promotion policies are those on:

❖ tariffs (which could affect government revenue and, in this way, impact on many policies);

❖ domestic subsidies (which could alter the feasibility of policies related to production and transfer entitlements);

❖ export subsidies (which could affect the feasibility of transfer and safety net policies).

In addition, multilateral rules on state trading enterprises and export regulation, as well as any new rules on process criteria, could have an impact.

Part 3

Trade Policy Reform and Food Security
Chapter 6: The Impact of the Uruguay Round

Part 2 has provided a shortlist of relatively cost-effective and efficient food security policies that might be affected by multilateral agricultural policy. Part 3 examines the evidence of whether such an effect has been felt as a result of the URAA or might be in prospect from the next multilateral Round.

6.1 The Provisions of the URAA

The Uruguay Round covered both tropical agriculture (coffee, cocoa, tea, sisal, palm oil, etc.) and temperate agriculture (wheat, sugar beet, milk, grapes, etc.). All of the earlier Rounds of tariff cutting included tropical agriculture, but a host of limitations and exceptions had allowed formidable protectionist barriers to be erected to trade in temperate products. The big – and controversial – innovation of the Uruguay Round was to extend coverage to temperate agriculture.

The terms *tropical* and *temperate* agriculture are imprecise ones. These geographical terms are used as a convenient shorthand description to divide the many agricultural products into two groups: those that have long been subject to GATT disciplines, and those that have been covered for the first time in the Uruguay Round. Tariffs have been cut on tropical products in the Uruguay Round, but were already low and so the changes are unlikely to have a major effect on food security.

Developing countries produce temperate as well as tropical products. Cereals and fruit/vegetables are the most important temperate items for developing countries (Figure 3). Moreover, some products of interest to developing countries are both tropical and temperate. Sugar, for example, can be produced either from cane (a tropical product) or beet (temperate). In WTO terminology, it tends to be referred to as a temperate product because it was not covered by agreed trade rules until the Uruguay Round.

What has been agreed on temperate agriculture is a compromise that will introduce normal market mechanisms into production and trade – but slowly. The main achievement of the Round was to begin the task of applying to agricultural trade the same sort of multilateral disciplines as have applied to manufactures for many years. In 2000 world trade in temperate agricultural goods is still significantly less liberal than is trade in manufactures [see Stevens *et al.* 1998 for further details].

Action was taken in three principal areas (with changes summarised in Table 9):

❖ domestic subsidies to agriculture (which have been classified into various categories of differing long-term legitimacy and subject to some reductions);

❖ market access (with most barriers converted into tariffs);

❖ export subsidies (which have been limited in relation both to the value of the subsidies given and the volume of exports that are subsidised).

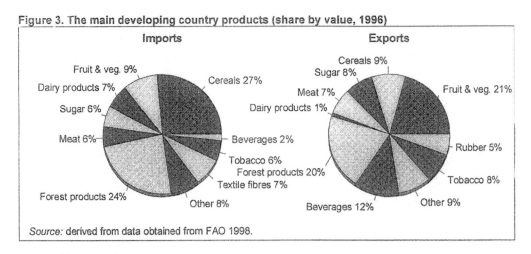

Figure 3. The main developing country products (share by value, 1996)

Imports
Fruit & veg. 9%
Dairy products 7%
Sugar 6%
Meat 6%
Forest products 24%
Cereals 27%
Beverages 2%
Tobacco 6%
Forest products 20%
Textile fibres 7%
Other 8%

Exports
Cereals 9%
Sugar 8%
Meat 7%
Dairy products 1%
Fruit & veg. 21%
Rubber 5%
Tobacco 8%
Other 9%
Beverages 12%

Source: derived from data obtained from FAO 1998.

Table 9 The Uruguay Round and agriculture: agreed cuts

Type of country	Agreed cuts in:			
	domestic subsidies	tariffs	export subsidies	volume of subsidised exports
Developed	20% over 6 years	36% over 6 years	36% over 6 years	21% over 6 years
Developing	13.3% over 10 years	24% over 10 years	24% over 10 years	14% over 10 years
Least developed	None	None	None	None

6.1.1 Domestic subsidies

As indicated in Table 8, the provisions on domestic subsidies could have a particularly important bearing on food security. The URAA was as much concerned to quantify and classify existing subsidies as it was to reduce them. In the process it introduced a structural distinction between the ways in which developed and developing country subsidies have been classified.

Since the ways in which governments (particularly in the developed world) have subsidised their agriculture are many, varied, and often opaque, the URAA provisions on domestic subsidies are also especially complex. As a first step to establish some common approach, each member was invited to calculate their total subsidies in the form of an Aggregate Measurement of Support (AMS) which applies to all supported commodities. All of the agreed cuts to domestic subsidies are expressed in terms of this AMS level. Evidently, the higher the base AMS

declared by a state and accepted by other WTO members, the greater the allowable subsidies after the agreed percentage cuts have been made. Most developing countries failed to submit substantial base AMSs in the URAA and, hence, their final AMS must be similarly modest (Figure 4).

Not all of the subsidies identified through this process need to be cut. They were classified into groups to determine whether or not they needed to be reduced and whether action could be taken against them under the WTO's dispute settlement mechanism. The categories established for the duration of the URAA are:

Exempt from reduction and non-actionable

❖ The **Green Box**: supports to agriculture which are deemed to be non-, or minimally, trade distorting. They do not need to be reduced under the Round, and the so-called Peace Clause (Article 13) is designed to limit the scope for other

WTO members to take action against them (such as the imposition of countervailing duties). Such supports include:

- publicly financed R&D;
- early retirement schemes for farmers;
- payments for long-term land retirement.

❖ The **Special and Differential Box** exempts from reduction: investment subsidies generally available to agriculture in developing countries; agricultural input subsidies generally available to low-income or resource-poor developing country producers; and anti-narcotic diversification incentives.

❖ The *de minimis* **provisions** of Article 6:4 exempt from reduction supports below a minimum threshold in any year. The cut-off point for developing countries (at 10% of production value) is double that applying to developed countries.

Exempt from reduction but actionable

❖ The **Blue Box**: direct payments under 'production limiting' programmes need not be cut but may be actionable by other WTO members.

To be reduced and actionable

❖ The **Amber Box** is a residual category of supports not covered by the three previous boxes (mainly product-specific supports and non-exempt subsidies) which must be reduced unless covered by the *de minimis* provisions.

Figure 4. Base and final levels of Aggregate Measurement of Support (AMS)

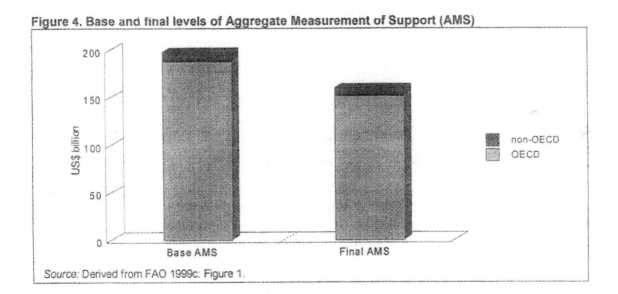

Source: Derived from FAO 1999c: Figure 1.

[Data not available   this was done 'by eye' from the source document]

Most developing countries put their faith in the SDT box and in the *de minimis* provision. They mainly failed to register any of their subsidies as falling within the Green Box or the Blue Box. Combined with their low AMS, this means that their continued scope for providing subsidies to their agriculture depends heavily on the extension of SDT.

6.1.2 Tariffs

Until the Uruguay Round the application of normal GATT disciplines to temperate agriculture was hedged with many exceptions and exclusions. Developed countries took advantage of these to create a complex array of measures to keep out imports. These often provided very high levels of protection to domestic producers which were additional to the direct and indirect subsidies included in the AMS. The EU's system of variable import levies for cereals and livestock products, for example, made it impossible for imports to undercut domestic producers: consumers were obliged to subsidise domestic production by paying higher prices that they would have done under a more liberal trade regime.

As a first step in applying to temperate agriculture the same sorts of disciplines as have long applied to industrial products most, but not all, of these different ways of restricting imports have been converted into tariffs. (Exceptions include, for example, the EU's entry price system for some fruit and vegetables.) A second step has been to 'bind' and then cut these tariffs (at the overall average rate set out in Table 9). Each contracting party has established a 'bound' (or maximum) tariff for every item and also agreed the date by which tariffs will be brought down from pre-Uruguay Round levels (known as 'base rates') to this new maximum.

But tariffication will not necessarily result in any major liberalisation. Even a cut of one-third from a very high level will still be a substantial import barrier. The contracting parties have considerable latitude in setting the level of these tariffs. The EU and most African states, for example, have set them at very high levels.

It is clear that these changes do not amount to 'substantial liberalisation'. This conclusion is reinforced by the consideration that members have been allowed to establish 'special safeguards' (SSGs) on specific products (which is how, for example, the EU justifies its entry prices system). Protection against exchange rate changes is given by the fact that import prices will be calculated in national currencies.

6.1.3 Export subsidies

In addition to the new rules on domestic taxpayer-funded subsidies and the subsidies paid by consumers through higher prices, the Uruguay Round also agreed specific reductions in export subsidies. This may assist developing country (and other) exporters in third markets where they have to compete with dumped developed country surpluses, but it may also increase the cost of supplies to food-importing developing countries.

Developed countries have agreed to reduce by 36% the *value* of direct export subsidies from their 1986 – 90 base level (often higher than current levels) and to cut the *quantity* of subsidised exports by 21% over six years. For developing countries, the reductions will be two-thirds of those applying to developed countries and the implementation period is extended to ten years. No reductions will need to be made by the least developed countries.

While significant, these cuts will still leave very substantial export subsidies in place. GATT has estimated the total level of export subsidies by developed countries in the base period as US$19 billion [GATT 1994]. Cereals, dairy products and meat receive the largest subsidies. Moreover, food aid and unsubsidised exports are not covered by these commitments.

6.2 Effects of the URAA on Food Security

The agreed changes affect all WTO members (including developing countries) in two ways. First, there are restrictions placed upon the policy freedom of governments; these might be called 'direct effects'. Certain policies that have been used in the past, or might be proposed for the future, may not now be available to governments. These effects are fairly easy to identify precisely.

The second type of effect, which could be called 'indirect effects', may be more substantial in the longer term but are much more difficult to identify precisely. One impact of the direct effects will be to alter world market conditions for agriculture. This is likely to provoke changes in both the level and the distribution of supply and demand. This will, in turn, alter the prices that some countries receive for their exports and pay for their imports. The broad scale of this has been sketched in Part 1, but the effects of partial liberalisation on particular items is a matter of speculation.

Both types of change have the potential to affect food security policies, even though on most counts this potential has not been realised. The provisions of the URAA did not 'bite' in the sense of producing substantial direct or indirect effects on developing countries that would impinge upon their food security policies. Nonetheless, the potential remains: there have been both direct and indirect effects of the Round and, by establishing the architecture for future negotiations, it may have a much greater medium-term impact if the next Round produces more substantial change.

The direct effects of the URAA on food security policies are clear (even though they are small): some of the activities analysed in Part 2 may become more or less feasible as a result of the Round. There will also be indirect effects: in cases where the efficiency, effectiveness or feasibility of a food security policy depends upon certain levels of imports or exports, then changes to these levels could be important.

6.2.1 Direct effects

The principal conclusion to be drawn from any analysis of the direct effects of the URAA is a reassuring one. The provisions do not substantially affect the freedom of manoeuvre of developing countries to undertake policies identified in Part 2 as desirable. The main area of concern arises from the *possibility* that the architecture established in the URAA could provide a framework for the future agreement of policies that would be more constraining. Although this is a danger that ought to be avoidable given due care and diligence, these will be forthcoming only if the problem is understood.

Architecture

The reason why the architecture established by the URAA could be problematic in future is that it does not adequately reflect developing country interests – a situation that has arisen because of the nature of the Uruguay Round negotiations. Much of the discussion on the URAA was between developed countries (and two in particular – the EU and the USA). Developing countries tended not to involve themselves and, in cases in which they felt that the proposed arrangements did not meet their interests, they tended to rely upon SDT examptions.

In consequence, the URAA contains substantial exemptions from the provisions on tariff and subsidy reduction, but most are available only to developed countries. This bias in the architecture of the Agreement has not yet had any substantial operational impact: the market access and subsidy targets agreed in the URAA are not constraining since the SDT and *de minimis* provisions are adequate. However, if the next Round were to result in an erosion of SDT provisions without any change in the architecture, the results could be more constraining for food security policies in developing countries. The effect could be particularly marked if the exemptions allowed in those parts of the agreement used mainly by developed countries were reduced by less than the SDT provisions available to developing countries. This could easily happen, given the WTO negotiating process, unless its avoidance is made a specific objective. The next chapter outlines some of the ways in which such an objective could be achieved.

Domestic subsidies

There is no evidence that food security policies have been constrained by the URAA commitments on domestic subsidies. Normally if there is inadequate government support to the activities identified in Part 2 the cause is more likely to be budgetary pressure (perhaps SAP-induced). But the case of India illustrates problems that could become more widespread in future and could have an effect on the feasibility of pursuing some of the policies described in Part 2. The food security impact of the problem in the particular case of India is uncertain (and is not investigated in this study). But it is easy to see from the example how governments might be constrained from pursuing desirable policies requiring public subsidy because of the legacy of past GATT commitments that may have been made without due foresight.

Because of controls on consumer prices India's product-specific total AMS for the base period (1986 – 88) was substantially negative – Rs 244 billion, or 22% of the total value of agricultural production [FAO 1999c]. Non-product-specific base period AMS, by contrast, was positive – but on a much smaller scale (Rs 46 billion or 4% of total value). While it has since increased (to 7.5% of total value) it still offsets to a very minor extent only the heavy product-specific tax of price controls. But since it can be justified in the URAA only under the *de minimis* provisions, which set a limit of 10%, India's scope for increasing further its preferred instrument of agricultural support is restricted. The SDT box cannot be used as a justification because the support is in the form of input subsidies and is not restricted to resource poor farmers.

Whilst the wisdom of widespread price con-

trols partly offset by subsidised inputs may be questioned, the point to be made is that the current URAA architecture does not in this case provide a neutral check on governments providing support that distorts trade by giving their farmers an unfair advantage over others. Instead, it has the effect of prescribing the ways in which agricultural policy is to be framed even in a country that, far from giving its farmers undue support, appears to be taxing them heavily. And the logical corollary is that if the URAA or its successor seeks to prescribe appropriate policies rather than concerning itself only with the net trade impact of a state's chosen regime then the text must include a detailed and comprehensive list of the policies deemed supportive of food security. And, as Part 2 has demonstrated, such a list could be very long and have many exceptions.

Direct effects on trade policy

The URAA requirements on domestic and export subsidies are unlikely to have restricted developing countries' freedom of manoeuvre (although, as is illustrated by the case of India, developing countries might face difficulties in the future). In many countries the URAA requirement to bind tariffs for all agricultural items was accommodated through the use of the 'once-and-for-all' opportunity to set their bound tariffs at high levels. The bound rates of the 14 out of the 17 states identified as particularly vulnerable in Part 1 for which data are available suggest that this has not had a significant effect on market access.

Figure 5 shows the distribution of cereals tariffs bound by the states identified in Table 5. The vast majority of lines have been bound at over 20%, with the 100 – 200% band containing the largest number. Since most of these states have been involved in SAPs, it is reasonable to conclude that few, if any, of these bound rates are close to the current applied rates. In the jargon, the bound tariffs have a lot of 'water' in them: they would only become a constraint on action if a government wished to raise its tariffs very considerably above current levels.

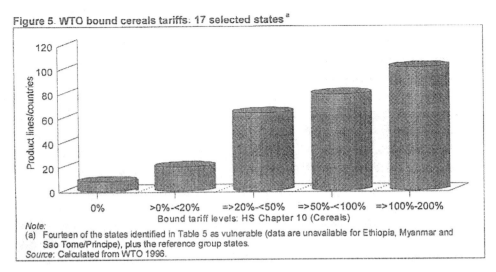

Figure 5. WTO bound cereals tariffs: 17 selected states [a]

Note:
(a) Fourteen of the states identified in Table 5 as vulnerable (data are unavailable for Ethiopia, Myanmar and Sao Tome/Principe), plus the reference group states.
Source: Calculated from WTO 1996.

In the case of developed countries, the device of high tariffs has been reinforced by the URAA provision on SSGs in Article 5. This allows additional duties to be imposed, but only on items which have been so designated in a member's schedules, if either the volume of imports exceeds a trigger level or their price falls below a trigger. The trigger thresholds are related to previous flows. Because developing countries, in the main, failed to register SSGs during the URAA negotiations, they do not have access to this device.

Developed countries have also used the provisions of Annex 5 to the URAA to maintain TRQs. Where tariffs have been set at such high levels as to be an effective barrier to access, TRQs (under which a reduced tariff applies to a set volume of imports) have been used to ensure a certain minimum level of access. In addition, pre-existing or new commitments to preferential suppliers (such as the EU's to New Zealand for butter and to some ACP states for sugar) have been covered by TRQs. The effect has been to favour some sources of supply over others to the regulated domestic markets of developed states applying TRQs. As explained in Part 1, this combination of protection and preference can have major effects on the trade-based entitlements of people in affected developing countries.

6.2.2 Indirect effects

Evidence of change

As explained in Part 1, the distortions that the URAA began to address have probably led to world prices for some commodities, including cereals, being lower than they would otherwise have been. Hence the erosion of the distortions could lead to a rise in world prices. A concern expressed during the Round was that food insecure developing countries might suffer adjustment problems from such a rise in world prices. *The Decision on Measures Concerning the Possible Negative Effects of the Reform Programme on Least-Developed and Net Food-importing Developing Countries* was drafted to take account of such concerns.

While the liberalisation of developed country agriculture was modest (with the result that it is unlikely to have had a major impact on the availability and price on the world market of commodities of importance (as exports or imports) to developing countries), there is some evidence that it has had limited effects. Moreover, there is evidence that the adjustment capacity of food-importing developing countries has deteriorated over the same period as a result of declining food aid volumes, even though this may not be related directly to the URAA.

An analysis by FAO [FAO 1999a] argues

that for some commodities the strengthening of trade flows and prices in 1995 – 7 was due, in a number of cases, partly to the implementation of the URAA commitments. It notes the cases of cereals and meat, in particular, in which some of the strengthening of the market was due to the reductions in export subsidies and domestic support and the opening of minimum levels of market access [FAO 1999a:5]. However, in the case of most other agricultural commodities the developments in the market over the 1995 – 7 period have had more to do with more 'traditional' factors such as weather and the commodity cycle. Developments since 1997, for all commodities, have been the result of factors that are unrelated to the URAA.

The FAO has also examined the possible effect of the URAA on price stability. It has found that there was no overall trend, and that while some of the changes observed during the 1995 – 7 period compared with earlier data would seem to be statistically significant it is unlikely that the cause was the URAA.

Although the URAA has not been a major factor, the changes in the world cereal market over the period since the Marrakech Agreement have been very difficult ones for LLDCs and NFIDCs. Their cereal import bill in 1995/6 was over 60% higher than the average for 1993/4 and 1994/5. Three-quarters of this increase was due to the rise in per unit costs rather than an increase in volume. A major reason is that the contribution of concessional imports has diminished substantially. During 1997/8, food aid in cereals accounted for 23% of LLDCs' cereal imports, compared with 36% in 1993/4; for the NFIDCs the relevant figures are 2% and 8%.

The record on adjustment support

The URAA *Decision on Measures Concerning the Possible Negative Effects of the Reform Programme on Least-Developed and Net Food-importing Developing Countries* was framed precisely to deal with such problems. However, little has been done under this heading. Both the IMF and the World Bank have indicated that they consider they have ade-quate resources within their normal programmes to deal with any adjustment problems arising from the URAA. And at the Singapore Ministerial Conference it was agreed that WTO members 'in their individual capacity as members of relevant international financial institutions' take appropriate steps to encourage necessary action 'through their respective governing bodies'.

In June 1999 a new Food Aid Convention (FAC) was approved for an initial three years. The volume of commitments, at 4.895 million tonnes of wheat equivalent, is lower than the level agreed under the old Convention of 5.35 million tonnes. But, in addition, the EC has agreed to provide €130 million in cash (claimed to be equivalent to 588,000 tonnes of wheat). At best, therefore, the new FAC maintains, but does not increase, food aid.

6.3 Summary

The overall effects of the URAA on food security policies are summarised in Table 10. This takes the types of useful food security policies identified in Part 2 (column 1), identifies the part of the URAA's architecture that is most relevant to their feasibility (column 2), and then specifies the provisions in the URAA that may be used to support such policies, distinguishing between those most and least used by developing countries. Those food security policies that involve direct government subsidies (such as input credits and food price stabilisation) can be pegged on the SDT and *de minimis* exemptions. Hence they have not been adversely affected to any substantial extent by the URAA. The role of tariffs in providing some degree of protection to domestic producers and government revenue (*inter alia* for food security expenditure) has also been maintained by the large amount of 'water' in developing country bound rates. The direct impact on feeding programmes of the URAA cuts in the subsidised exports of (mainly) developed countries has been small, but since it has occurred in the context of sharp falls in food aid the pain may have been greater than would appear from the aggregate figures.

Table 10 Provisions relating to food security in the URAA

Food security policies	Related WTO trade policy area	URAA provisions available to developing countries		URAA effect
		Widely used	*Not widely used*	
Input credits and subsidies; capital expenditure in agriculture; food price stabilisation and subsidies	Domestic subsidies	SDT exemptions from cuts in agricultural investment and input subsidies for poor farmers 10% *de minimis* exemption LLDCs exempt from any cuts	Green Box Substantial base AMS	Limited
All policies involving government expenditure; export development; protection to domestic farmers	Tariffs	High bound rates containing 'water' Lower (for developing) and zero (for least developed) tariff cutting obligations	SSGs TRQs	Limited
Labour-intensive public works and targeted feeding programmes; food stamps	Export subsidies	Food aid exempt from developed country reduction commitments		Limited but relatively important for vulnerable states in context of food aid cutback

At the same time, it is clear that there are several other substantial pegs on which food security policies might have been justified, but which are not usable in practice by developing countries that failed to take the necessary steps during the URAA. This is not a problem for food security – provided that the pegs available to developing countries remain adequate for the task. They would become inadequate either through some variation of 'the India problem' noted above or through the erosion of SDT or *de minimis* provisions in future negotiations.

Chapter 7: The Next Multilateral Agricultural Round

7.1 Origins

As noted, while the great achievement of the Uruguay Round was to bring temperate agriculture into the same broad framework of rules as other merchandise, the price was that substantial liberalisation of trade in the sector was deferred. The WTO members will soon turn their attention to this unfinished business.

The URAA contains several commitments that will lead to a new set of negotiations on multilateral liberalisation. The most basic is Article 20 of the URAA, which commits countries to work towards further substantial progressive reductions in support and protection to agriculture and contains a timetable which led to the resumption of negotiations in March 2000.

In addition to Article 20, there are a number of other provisions in the URAA that effectively make further negotiations essential. Article 5 covers the duration of the SSG provisions. While there is some disagreement over the interpretation to be given to this article, some analysts argue that the existing SSGs would lapse if progress on further reform were to falter.[3] Annex 5 of the URAA allows a small number of countries to avoid tariffication by offering higher market access commitments (with Japan and Korea the most notable examples). This provision will lapse unless extended through negotiation.

The URAA provision that is widely perceived to be the most important stimulus to a further Agreement is Article 13 – the Peace Clause. Although doubt has been cast on the exact meaning of Article 13, it is commonly held to stop members from bringing challenges against export subsidies, the Green and Blue Boxes, and domestic *de minimis* supports until 2003-4 when it expires. The interpretation implies that current practices, which are not being challenged at the moment, could be subject to challenge after the Peace Clause expires. It follows that countries vulnerable to such challenge will have an incentive to conclude such negotiations on a successor agreement to the URAA before the deadline of 2003 – 4.

In addition to these built-in legal reasons for a new set of negotiations, there is perceived to be a need to deal with various problems that have arisen during the period since the URAA was negotiated. These include the administration of TRQs, the domestic support reduction commitments, compliance with export subsidy commitments, and market access provisions. In addition, there is a wide range of issues that are labelled 'non-trade concerns'. These include, most importantly for the present study, food security which, as noted, tends to be considered in the WTO context to be concerned particularly with the availability of food imports.

Not least, there is widespread pressure to liberalise agriculture further. This includes pressure from consumer and budgetary sources even in the EU. The Cairns Group, in particular, has expressed a strong desire that the next Round result in substantial reductions in export subsidies (their highest priority), followed by improved market access.

The new Round, which began in March 2000, is likely to involve a substantial increase in

---

3   FAO 1999b: this section relies heavily upon this source.

the level of trade liberalisation compared with what was agreed in the Uruguay Round. The timetable for the completion of the negotiations is uncertain, as is their form, but a number of 'milestones' can be identified. Of these, 2003 – 4 (when the Peace Clause expires) is the most powerful.

Preliminary skirmishing on the agenda is already occurring under the organisational framework of the WTO Analysis and Information Exchange on Agriculture (AIE). Although such exchanges are not in any way binding, they provide some insight into the range of issues that WTO members will wish to raise during the negotiations that are anticipated to get fully under way early in 2000.

7.2 Possible Areas of Negotiation

Since the negotiations have yet to commence, any review of the items on the agenda, let alone the results, must be speculative. However, there seems to be a consensus that the URAA has established the central architecture for multilateral rules. In other words, the agenda for the next Round is likely to take the form of parallel discussions under each of the main URAA headings. These are: domestic support, market access, and export subsidies.

7.2.1 Domestic support

Although the rules on domestic subsidies are those with the greatest potential implications for the food security policies of developing countries, there is not a great deal of detailed guidance available at present on the likely agenda. There is likely to be pressure to reduce total AMS levels in the next Round, to change the composition of the multicoloured boxes and to alter the rules pertaining to them.

There is expected in particular to be negotiations around a reduction in the Blue Box supports. However, the situation of the main protagonists is becoming less clear-cut. It had been assumed that the USA's FAIR Act had allowed it to reclassify all of its supports in a way that would obviate a continued need for the Blue Box. It had been expected, therefore, to join with Cairns Group states to push for the elimination of Blue Box supports that cannot be absorbed into a country's *de minimis* exemption. The EU, by contrast, continues to require Blue Box support even with the full implementation of *Agenda 2000* [see Swinbank *et al.* 1999]. In recent years, however, the USA has introduced a raft of new subsidies which would appear to be challengeable without the retention of the Blue Box. Hence the next Round may not see the USA ranged with the Cairns Group and against the EU, as had earlier been expected.

In any case, these negotiations would have a less direct effect on food security policies than would any change in SDT (including the higher *de minimis* exemption available to developing countries). This is because of the different location in the URAA texts of developed and developing country subsidies (see Chapter 6). There does not seem to be any consensus on what may happen to SDT. There does not appear to be any major challenge to the concept of LLDCs, but this group does not overlap exactly with countries in which food security may be influenced by the outcome of the next Round (see Part 2).

7.2.2 Market access

There is somewhat more guidance to be had on the market access issues likely to be raised. There will be moves to reduce the 'water' in current bound tariffs and to extend, if not complete, the process of tariffication by reducing TRQs and SSGs. Although a reduction in tariffs is considered highly likely, there is no guidance to be had at the present time as to whether the approach will be the Uruguay Round formula (e.g. 15% per product minimum, with 36% on average); an across-the-board gradual tariff cut; the establishment of a fixed maximum for all products (e.g. no tariffs higher than 50%); or the 'Swiss formula' which involves steeper reductions for higher rates. There may also be moves to reduce tariff escalation and the dispersion of tariff rates.

The special derogations under Annex 5 which allowed some countries to use TRQs to limit tariffication for certain commodities are likely to come under pressure. This may include both a reduction in the scope of TRQs and changes in their administration. Because of problems that have arisen with the administration of TRQs, there is likely to be pressure for improved transparency in the administration and monitoring of them, their allocation to preferential suppliers (with implications *inter alia* for the EU's Sugar and Banana Protocols), the allocation of TRQs to state trading enterprises or producer organisations, the auctioning of licences for TRQs, and conditionalities imposed upon TRQ beneficiaries.

The outcome of negotiations is impossible to determine, but the complete elimination of TRQs appears to be unlikely. Rather, there will be pressure for them to be recognised as transitory and to reduce their impact through a variety of possible mechanisms. These could include raising minimum access levels, and eliminating the 'water' in the tariff that applies in excess of the quota.

The trade-related entitlements of those states affected positively or negatively by the TRQs may be altered by such changes. Although it is premature to attempt an identification, let alone a quantification, of such changes, the 'worst outcome' would be one in which the erosion of 'rents' for the favoured states (e.g. via the EU's Sugar or Beef Protocols) is not offset by substantial improvements in market access allowing exporters to recoup the fall in prices via an increase in the volume of sales.

7.2.3 Export subsidies

The practice of subsidising agricultural exports is very heavily concentrated: only 25 of the 135 WTO members have a right to subsidise exports,

and the bulk of subsidies are paid by two or three exporters [FAO 1999b]. Three exporters account for 93% of subsidised exports of wheat, while for beef and butter the relevant figures are two exporters, and respectively 80% and 94% of subsidies.

Because of this limited number of countries with an interest in continuing the URAA tolerance of subsidised exports, it is likely that this is an area on which pressure for change will be substantial. Indeed, the members of the Cairns Group consulted during this study indicated that their highest priority for the next Round is the elimination of export subsidies.

A reduction in export subsidies would tend to have a greater impact on food security as conventionally defined within WTO circles than it would in relation to the concept as defined in this Report. To that extent it is possible that the dangers to food security of change in this area will be exaggerated by analysts and opinion-formers close to the negotiations. Nonetheless, there are potential negative effects (mainly of a short-to-medium-term nature) for those types of food security (on the broad definition used in this Report) that make use of subsidised imports.

7.3 Food Security Interests

The implications of such change for the food security policies identified in Part 2 are summarised in Table 11. For each of the three main parts of the URAA architecture (column 1), the table identifies the types of change currently being mooted (column 2). Each of these changes has the potential to affect the feasibility of desirable food security policies. Whilst it is not helpful in advance of the negotiations to provide what would be, effectively, guesses on the likelihood of this potential being realised, it is useful to sketch some of the ways in which food security might be protected in the event of change. Some of the options are listed in column 3.

Table 11 Potential issues for the next Round

Changes that could affect food security		Potential alternative instruments
Policy area	*Types of change*	
Domestic subsidies	Erosion of SDT provisions on investment and input subsidies Cut in *de minimis* provisions	Recalculation of AMS Redesign of Green Box
Tariffs	Removal of 'water' from tariffs before end of developed country subsidised production	Provision of SSGs Countervailing duties
Export subsidies	Reduction of subsidised imports available to *vulnerable* countries and groups that is more rapid than feasible adjustment	Targeting of concessional food (possibly outside WTO framework)

7.3.1 Domestic subsidies

There is a common view in developed country circles that SDT is undesirable and, for this reason alone, there may be pressure to limit the current provisions on domestic subsidies. Regardless of the general merits of the SDT concept, the argument of this paper is that in the URAA they are the corollary of the developing countries' exclusion from the substantial subsidy exemptions available to developed countries through their Green Box and AMS provisions. Hence, any moves to erode SDT, or the linked higher *de minimis* provisions, should be accompanied by offsetting changes to the Green Box and/or AMS arrangements.

What form such Green Box changes should take is open to two approaches. One would be to make a simple but broad provision, similar to the current SDT approach, that approves expenditure that is normal for developing countries and helps poor farmers. The other approach is to argue that since such a formulation would be open to potential abuse it should be limited through a much more specific set of exemptions. But the analysis of Part 2 suggests that such a list would need to be extensive and detailed if it were not to risk placing undesirable obstacles in the path of food security.

Such a list may be difficult to negotiate. The developing country group includes a wide range of countries, and the richer members are unlikely to be willing to agree graduation (which they can presumably block under WTO consensus procedures). And neither the LLDC nor NFIDC groups overlap completely with the countries that are food insecure on the broad definition used in this study. Hence, the provision of important concessions to particular food insecure types of developing country in the next Round may depend upon the creation of new operationally useful classifications of sub-groups within the WTO.

If it becomes desirable (in the context of SDT erosion) to revisit the AMS calculations of the URAA, there are a number of possible ways to resolve the specific problems that could arise from the failure of developing countries to register positive base levels. It is beyond the scope of this study to assess whether any are intrinsically superior to others, and probably unnecessary so far in advance of the emergence of a specific problem to be resolved. With this caveat, it can be argued that the best approach is likely to be the one that is politically most feasible to negotiate. Among the avenues would be to allow developing countries to recalculate their

AMSs; to raise their *de minimis* levels across the board or, at least, for basic foodstuffs; to give credit for negative AMS for food security purposes; and to exempt from AMS/*de minimis* calculations expenditures which are strictly on food security (such as for food security stocks).

7.3.2 Market access

If part of a genuine liberalisation of world agricultural trade, cuts in bound tariffs rates to reduce or eliminate 'water' would normally be considered to be a desirable move. But it is most unlikely that the next Round will result in a completely liberal agricultural trading system, with the result that substantial distortions will remain. For this reason liberalisation by food insecure states may not be so straightforward. A particular cause for concern will arise if the Round were to result in reductions in developing country tariffs that are more rapid than the removal of production and export subsidies in developed states.

As long as developed country subsidies remain, prices in the world market will not necessarily reflect production costs. The extent to which world prices are below true market clearing levels is indicated by the estimates of how much they would rise following liberalisation (summarised in Table 4). It is far from clear that it is economically desirable for developing countries to open up their domestic markets to items from other countries that are sold at below the cost of production. And from the entitlements approach to food security it is likely often to be very undesirable to permit serious damage to be done to domestic agriculture in poor countries by imports that have been dumped. This applies regardless of whether or not this is the direct result of subsidies by the exporter or simply a consequence of non-subsidising producers being forced to match the 'market prices' created by the subsidies (domestic or export) of their competitors.

There are a number of plausible ways in which food security policies can be defended from such distortions. The key factor determin-ing their relative desirability is likely to be the feasibility of reaching a consensus within the WTO rather than the intrinsic merits of the schemes themselves. Among possible candidates are: extension of SSGs to more developing countries; the retention of relatively high bound tariffs on temperate agricultural products; and the use of countervailing duty procedures until trade-distorting developed country subsidies have been eliminated.

Largely by omission rather than design, developing countries registered few SSGs under the Uruguay Round. It could be argued that the simplest way to deal with the subsidy problem is to rectify this imbalance in the next Round. The political and economic concerns of developing countries, which might deter them from agreeing to reduce tariffs, could be alleviated if tariff reduction were accompanied by the explicit provision of SSGs on items likely to be subject to trade-distorting subsidies in developed countries.

The most direct alternative would be to exempt developing countries (or the food insecure ones) from tariff cuts on the items most likely to be subject to subsidised world trade. The problem with this approach is that it would extend rather than reduce differentiation within agriculture, when an avowed aim of both the URAA and its successor is to establish consistent, universal rules.

Countervailing duties are an instrument that can be used to protect domestic farmers from subsidised imports. But this route has its problems. First, the proliferation and misuse of anti-dumping actions are widely deemed to be corrosive of the international rule-based trading system. It is desirable, *ceteris paribus*, to reduce rather than aggravate the use of such measures. In addition, countervailing and anti-dumping actions are not, in practice, available to the poorer developing countries. This is because, in order to guarantee immunity from challenge, complex and rigorous administrative and legal procedures have to be followed in the implementation of anti-dumping and countervailing actions. These are beyond the capacities and legal systems of many developing countries. Whilst they could still impose countervailing levies, their willingness to do so is likely to be dampened by the knowledge that they could be vulnerable to a complaint by an aggrieved party.

7.3.3 Export subsidies

The reduction, and quite possibly elimination, of export subsidies will be a high priority in the next Round. Developing country policies that involve the provision of cheap food to enhance the trade-based or transfer entitlements of the food insecure and which rely upon imports to deliver supplies, in whole or in part, are likely to be made less feasible if the substantial subsidies still given by two or three major exporters are removed as a result of the next Round.

In principle this should be an area in which food security needs can be assured. Even if the next Round results in the elimination of export subsidies, this is likely to occur over an adjustment period. The complete disappearance of subsidised exports, therefore, may be up to ten years away.

This allows a reasonable period of time for making provision either to alter existing food security policies that depend upon subsidised imported foods or to make alternative financing arrangements. One plausible method for reconciling the desirability of reducing export subsidies with the need for a reasonable adjustment period for food security would be to establish different rates of subsidy reduction, depending on whether the items were destined for a food insecure country or more generally.

But the experience on implementation of the URAA suggests that it will require greater effort. The failure to take any serious action under the URAA *Decision on Measures Concerning the Possible Negative Effects of the Reform Programme on Least Developed and Net Food-importing Developing Countries* and the precipitate fall in food aid to LLDCs and NFIDCs provide no cause for complacency. It is clear that, whatever the cause (and the URAA is not a major one), the poorest and most food insecure countries have been required to make major adjustments to a sharp decline of food aid availability over a very short period of time. Such sharp cuts are not compatible with the orderly adjustment of food security policies.

Chapter 8: Conclusions

The main conclusion of the study is that it should be possible to reconcile the objective of international agricultural liberalisation with the pursuit of effective food security policies in developing countries, but that this will require an explicit effort to achieve. The URAA laid foundations for common rules to international trade that are likely to be built upon in the next Round beginning in the year 2000. Whilst the outcome of these negotiations is a matter of speculation, there are reasons to expect that decisions taken in the area of export subsidies, market access and domestic subsidies could have implications for desirable food security policies.

8.1 Trade Policy and Food Security

The rules on the agricultural trade policies of *states* affect the food security of *individuals*, but often indirectly. Food security is defined as *enough* food for an active healthy life; *access* to this food; and the *guarantee* of having access to it at any given time. Government actions defined as *food security policies*, which are the primary focus of this study, are those designed to promote or protect the different sources of 'entitlements' to food security. The policies considered most useful and feasible are those concerned with:

* food production (e.g. input credit and subsidies, capital expenditure and investment promotion);

* marketing (e.g. market development, parastatal reform and food price stabilisation);

* labour (e.g. promotion of high-value export crops and small and medium enterprises);

* transfers and safety nets (e.g. labour-

intensive public works programmes and targeted feeding programmes).

The food security of individuals is thus affected by a much wider range of factors than those that will be involved in the next Round of agricultural trade liberalisation. The definition of 'food security' commonly used within the WTO context is much narrower. It is often taken to relate primarily to the adequate supply of imported food to member states. Domestic policies that affect production, trade, labour and transfer entitlements are much more important absolutely for the food security of individuals than is international trade policy. Even to the extent that food security is affected by international trade policy, the impact will often be in the non-food sector (for example, by altering the trade- and labour-based entitlements of workers in manufacturing).

This report has been concerned, therefore, with a small subset of the issues of, on the one hand, food security and, on the other, international trade rule making and liberalisation. But it is an important area. The massive growth in international trade in food products over the last three decades and the dependence of some food security policies on the current rules for international trade mean that certain desirable practices currently undertaken could become less feasible if the next agricultural trade Round were to result in poorly drafted rules.

8.2 The Next WTO Round

All of the main sources of food security entitlement could be affected by the next agricultural trade Round, which may:

* introduce change to the policies (of both

domestic and foreign governments) that impact on the level of entitlements (for example, by altering the food prices paid by consumers or received by producers);

❖ make more or less feasible some of the policies that are considered desirable to promote or protect entitlements.

Current expectations are that the next agricultural trade Round will cover three main areas — export subsidies, market access and domestic subsidies. All three have the potential to impinge upon food security either:

❖ directly, by establishing new rules on food security policies currently in place or recommended in vulnerable developing countries; or

❖ indirectly, by altering absolute and relative agricultural prices which will, in turn, change entitlements.

These three areas have been listed in the order in which most change is anticipated. But in terms of the likely impact on food security, the priority order is different. It is domestic subsidies, tariffs and export subsidies.

There is thus an asymmetry between the areas likely to have the greatest impact on food security and those anticipated, at present, to feature most prominently in the negotiations. This explains why the next WTO Round may not have major effects, for good or ill, on food security. One consequence is that positive effects cannot simply be assumed to result (for example from developed country liberalisation), but another is that it ought to be feasible to identify modalities that will prevent serious adverse effects. The prime requirement for this second outcome is that negotiators are informed about the implications of proposed change for the entitlements of the food insecure.

The conclusion from this study is that there is no overwhelming reason to suppose that it will be difficult to achieve a balance in the new rules between the desirable objectives of extending robust disciplines to international trade in temperate agricultural products and fostering sensible food security policies. Given the uncertainty over the negotiating agenda, let alone the extent to which agreement can be reached, it is not possible to make any estimate of the potential effects of the next Round. But a number of desirable guidelines can be identified.

❖ Developing countries should have sufficient time and support to introduce alternative revenue sources.

❖ The erosion of rents in protected OECD markets in which developing countries receive preferences should be achieved principally by increased market access rather than through cuts in administered prices. This is because enhanced access for imports would tend to reduce prices in the protected market (by increasing supply relative to demand), but would do so in a way that allowed efficient exporters to increase sales. Cuts in administered prices without market opening, by contrast, simply result in a revenue loss to the favoured exporters without any beneficial shift in the international division of labour.

❖ The production and trade entitlements of farmers should be protected from dumped imports. The means by which this is to be achieved is less important than the objective.

❖ The URAA established a distinction in SDT between developing countries and the LLDC sub-group. But the latter is not an entirely satisfactory category for identifying food insecure states. If SDT for the broader category of developing countries is reduced, a new sub-category of food insecure states may be desirable.

❖ The institutional asymmetry between provisions for developed and developing country subsidies should be resolved in a way that recognises that it is often desirable from the perspective of food security to have production-related government support in insecure states.

But the nature of WTO negotiations means that such outcomes will not happen automatically. The results of the Round will be what the members of the WTO *negotiate*. And these negotiations will be between states of unequal negotiating power. A requirement for a successful integration of international trade rules and food security policies, therefore, is the informed participation of vulnerable countries in the negotiations. This requires *inter alia* two things which may involve action by developed countries:

❖ the provision of appropriate technical and financial assistance to enable those WTO developing country members that wish to participate in the negotiations to do so effectively;

❖ the exercise by developed countries of, in the WTO jargon, 'due restraint' in the negotiations to ensure that the concerns of developing countries are registered and not squeezed out by an over-concentration on issues of direct concern only to a small number of very important agricultural trading states.

Appendix 1: Identifying Vulnerable States

The Relative Importance of Agricultural Imports

Agriculture's share of total imports

Big countries will tend to import more than small countries, but that does not indicate whether or not they are more dependent on imports. One shorthand method to obtain a flavour of the countries that appear to have proportionally high agricultural imports is to examine agriculture's share of their total imports. This exercise has been undertaken using FAO data for 1994 on all developing countries listed.

The countries in which agriculture accounts for 20% or more by value are listed in Table 1.1. There are 44 such countries. Although all but 13 of them have agricultural imports that are one-third or less of the total, this is still a very high percentage. The average for the world, for developed countries, and for developing countries as a group is only 9%. Hence, even the lower cut-off of 20% represents a proportion that is over twice the average.

Table 1.1 The sectoral composition of imports

Country	Imports 1994 ($ million)			Agricultural trade as a share of total	Cereals as a share of agricultural trade
	Total	Agricultural	Cereals & preparations		
Haiti	252	207	92	82%	44%
Sierra Leone	151	94	44	62%	47%
Mauritania	240	140	45	58%	32%
Guinea-Bissau	63	33	20	52%	61%
Congo, Dem. Rep.	383	180	80	47%	44%
Somalia	200	89	33	45%	37%
Liberia	210	83	47	40%	57%
Djibouti	225	87	19	39%	22%
Cape Verde	170	65	18	38%	28%
Comoros	53	20	8	38%	40%
Gambia	210	78	30	37%	38%
Malawi	428	155	127	36%	82%
Iraq	1,900	684	215	36%	31%
Senegal	1,154	386	135	33%	35%
Tuvalu	6	2	0	33%	0%
Afghanistan	370	123	65	33%	53%
Myanmar	878	288	8	33%	3%

Country	Imports 1994 ($ million)			Agricultural trade as a share of total	Cereals as a share of agricultural trade
	Total	Agricultural	Cereals & preparations		
Tonga	69	69	3	32%	14%
Algeria	10,151	3,142	1,330	31%	42%
Niger	370	112	42	30%	38%
Central African Rep.	150	45	18	30%	40%
São Tome/Principe	24	7	3	29%	43%
Yemen	3,000	843	301	28%	36%
Kiribati	36	10	3	28%	30%
Cuba	2,200	604	195	27%	32%
Egypt	10,185	2,760	1,122	27%	41%
Rwanda	350	94	33	27%	35%
Samoa	80	21	4	26%	19%
Guinea	688	177	80	26%	45%
Sudan	1,170	296	160	25%	54%
Grenada	119	30	6	25%	20%
Mongolia	223	55	21	25%	38%
Libya	4,340	1,033	364	24%	35%
St Lucia	300	70	12	23%	17%
Jordan	3,381	772	188	23%	24%
St Vincent/Grenadines	135	30	12	22%	40%
Nicaragua	786	168	58	21%	35%
Benin	502	105	33	21%	31%
Ethiopia	1,033	215	165	21%	77%
Suriname	265	55	8	21%	15%
Vanuatu	92	19	6	21%	32%
Angola	1,633	336	91	21%	27%
Burundi	224	45	26	20%	58%
Oman	4,012	787	105	20%	13%
World	4,265,476	395,603	50,768	9%	13%
Developed countries	3,070,799	287,602	26,771	9%	9%
Developing countries	1,194,676	108,000	23,997	9%	22%

Source: FAO 1996.

The table also shows cereal imports as a proportion of total agricultural imports. The reason for this is to demonstrate that for many countries cereals represent an important agricultural import: for 26 of the 44 countries listed in the table the share of cereals is greater than one-third, and for seven of these it is over one-half; in only seven is it less than one-fifth.

This is an important operational point for the research. The share of agriculture in total imports is, of course, only a very indirect indicator of vulnerability. It has been selected primarily because of the ease with which comparable data can be collected. What is much more important is the share of total supply that is accounted for by imports. But it is not easy to show this at an aggregate level: because of their different weights, the volume of imports/domestic production of different agricultural goods cannot sensibly be aggregated. Similarly, because of very different unit values the value of imports/domestic production cannot sensibly be aggregated.

Food balance sheets

If it is accepted that cereals, a relatively homogenous product group, can be taken as a rough proxy for all basic foods, this methodological difficulty can be overcome. FAO food balance sheets allow a direct comparison to be made between the relative importance of imports and domestic production in a country's total food supply. The balance sheets for 1996 of all listed developing countries have been analysed from this perspective.

The results of this analysis of FAO food balance sheets are presented in Table 1.2. The top half of Table 1.2 lists those countries identified in Table 1.1. In 20 of these, imports account for over 50% of domestic cereals supply. This compares with a global average of 14%, and an average for developing countries as a whole of 13%.

The bottom half of Table 1.2 lists other developing countries (which were not picked up in the analysis that produced Table 1.1) in which imports also account for 50% or more of total supply.

Table 1.2 Cereals food balance sheets

Country	Domestic supply: cereals ex. beer, 1996 (1000 metric tons)					Imports as share of total
	Production	Imports	Stock change	Exports	Total	
Countries in Table 1.1:						
St Vincent/Grenadines	1	43	0	25	19	226%
Grenada	0	25	0	4	21	119%
Kiribati	0	12	-1	0	11	109%
St Lucia	0	26	-3	0	24	108%
Vanuatu	1	12	1	0	13	92%
Cape Verde	10	70	-1	0	79	89%
Jordan	99	1,465	184	2	1,746	84%
Libya	321	1,635	53	0	2,009	81%
Cuba	341	1,356	1	0	1,699	80%
Liberia	63	213	0	0	276	77%
Djibouti	0	57	16	0	74	77%
Yemen	664	2,045	83	0	2,792	73%
Comoros	15	36	4	0	55	65%
Rwanda	181	290	0	0	472	61%
Mauritania	210	287	-29	0	468	61%
Angola	522	560	-150	0	932	60%
Haiti	356	536	15	0	907	59%
Såo Tome/Principe	4	8	2	0	14	57%
Sierra Leone	314	308	-21	0	600	51%
Gambia	98	102	0	0	200	51%
Senegal	927	740	62	1	1,727	43%

Country	Domestic supply: cereals ex. beer, 1996 (1000 metric tons)					Imports as share of total
	Production	Imports	Stock change	Exports	Total	
Algeria	4,902	3,850	583	3	9,330	41%
Guinea-Bissau	134	74	0	0	208	36%
Egypt	14,912	7,767	360	330	22,709	34%
Guinea	645	298	-1	0	942	32%
Mongolia	219	135	85	0	440	31%
Nicaragua	616	231	1	11	836	28%
Iraq	2,910	1,068	-39	0	3,938	27%
Suriname	147	36	22	69	137	26%
Somalia	289	112	50	0	452	25%
Congo, Dem. Rep.	1,485	318	85	0	1,888	17%
Malawi	1,919	325	-230	10	2,005	16%
Burundi	259	46	11	0	316	15%
Benin	660	107	48	0	816	13%
Central African Rep.	133	19	9	0	161	12%
Sudan	5,201	449	-195	380	5,076	9%
Ethiopia	10,928	451	-1,250	0	10,129	4%
Niger	2,320	115	183	0	2,619	4%
Afghanistan	3,445	156	0	0	3,602	4%
Myanmar	12,452	35	-460	197	11,830	0%
Oman	n/a	n/a	n/a	n/a	n/a	n/a
Samoa	n/a	n/a	n/a	n/a	n/a	n/a
Tonga	n/a	n/a	n/a	n/a	n/a	n/a
Tuvalu	n/a	n/a	n/a	n/a	n/a	n/a
Other countries with high import dependence:						
UAE	7	1,293	-189	499	612	211%
Fiji Islands	15	191	-62	10	133	144%
Kuwait	2	603	13	130	488	124%
Mauritius	0	292	0	40	252	116%
Brunei Darussalam	1	54	-7	0	47	115%
Maldives	0	40	-3		37	108%
Barbados	2	78	-1	6	73	107%
Trinidad/Tobago	11	280	0	19	273	103%
St Kitts/Nevis		5	0		5	100%
Antigua/Barbuda	0	6	0	0	6	100%
Dominica	0	9	0	0	9	100%
Seychelles		15	1	0	16	94%
Jamaica	4	308	25	5	332	93%
Bahamas	0	24	3	0	26	92%
Solomon Islands	0	30	3	0	33	91%
Costa Rica	149	724	-11	40	823	88%
Bermuda		6	0		7	86%
Lebanon	74	854	74	0	1,001	85%
Congo, Rep.	20	114	0	0	134	85%
Malaysia	1,381	4,385	-91	371	5,305	83%
Cyprus	141	593	-4	3	727	82%
Papua New Guinea	3	276	68	0	347	80%

Country	Domestic supply: cereals ex. beer, 1996 (1000 metric tons)					Imports as share of total
	Production	Imports	Stock change	Exports	Total	
Gabon	31	116	0	0	147	79%
Lesotho	256	339	-135	1	459	74%
Dominican Rep.	377	1,002	0	2	1,377	73%
Botswana	83	180	-3	9	250	72%
Korea Rep.	5,244	12,403	495	113	18,030	69%
Venezuela	1,990	2,352	-518	155	3,670	64%
Namibia	87	139	0		226	62%
Saudi Arabia	1,880	6,017	2,466	22	10,341	58%
Peru	1,940	2,480	-120	7	4,293	58%
Colombia	2,895	3,283	-350	43	5,785	57%
Panama	273	323	9	5	600	54%
Eritrea	124	245	120	0	489	50%
World	1,885,790	256,456	-33,509	251,025	1,857,712	14%
Developed countries	861,726	110,351	-24,109	216,416	731,552	15%
Developing countries	1,024,064	146,105	-9,400	34,609	1,126,160	13%

Source: FAO 1999d.

Assessing Vulnerability

The criteria

The countries listed in Table 1.2 provide an initial population of states that are heavily reliant on imports, but not all are necessarily vulnerable (Malaysia and Saudi Arabia, for example). The list needs to be refined further to identify from this import-dependent group the states that could be considered especially vulnerable to change (including that induced by international trade policy).

A range of plausible criteria could be identified for such refining. Additional features of trade and production could be used, but it is argued that this would be relatively unlikely to improve greatly our understanding at such an aggregate level of analysis. Instead, the next step adopted in the study was to apply criteria related to the broader economic vulnerability of countries. These take account both of the national income of the state and also the volatility of economic activity. The exercise is based on work undertaken by the Commonwealth Secretariat.

The two criteria that have been employed for selection are:

❖ low real GDP *per capita*;

❖ vulnerability.

For the first criterion we selected the 25 poorest countries in Commonwealth Secretariat /World Bank [1999], Table 2. In addition, for the second we selected from among the next 25 poorest countries those that were also among the 25 most vulnerable, as measured by the composite vulnerability index [*ibid.*]. In other words, we selected the poorest countries and then a group of quite poor and very vulnerable countries. Since completing the exercise the Commonwealth Secretariat have developed the index further [see Easter 1999].

References

Abbott, J. 1987. *Agricultural Marketing Enterprises for the Developing World*. Cambridge: Cambridge University Press.

Alderman, H. and von Braun, J. 1984. 'The Effects of the Egyptian Subsidy System on Income Distribution and Consumption', *Research Report* 45 (July). Washington DC: International Food Policy Research Institute.

Amin, N. 1990. *Peasant Differentiation and Food Security in Zimbabwe*. New York: The Project.

Anderson, K. and Tyers, R. 1991. 'Effects of gradual food policy reforms following the Uruguay Round', *European Review of Agricultural Economics*, 19(1): January.

Baulch, B. 1999. 'Food Marketing' in S. Devereux (ed.) *Food Security in Africa: A Reader* (forthcoming).

Besley, T. and Kanbur, R. 1993. 'The Principles of Targeting', in M. Lipton and J. van der Gaag (eds) *Including the Poor: Proceedings of a Symposium Organised by the World Bank and the International Food Policy Research Institute*. Washington DC: The World Bank.

Brown, M. and Goldin, I. 1992. *The Future of Agriculture: Developing Country Implications*. Paris: OECD Development Centre.

Christensen, G. and Stack, J. 1992. 'The dimensions of household food insecurity in Zimbabwe, 1980 – 91'. Queen Elizabeth House, Food Studies Group.

Christiaensen, L. 1995. *Food Security: From Concept to Action*. Leuven: Catholic University of Leuven.

Commonwealth Secretariat/World Bank 1999. 'Small States: A Composite Vulnerability Index. First Draft'. Paper prepared by the Joint Commonwealth Secretariat/World Bank Task Force for the 'Conference on the Small States', St Lucia, West Indies, February 17 – 19 1999.

Cornia, G. and Stewart, F. 1995. 'Two Errors of Targeting', in D. van der Walle and K. Nead (eds) *Public Spending and the Poor: Theory and Evidence*. Washington DC: The World Bank.

Cromwell, E. 1992. 'Malawi', in A. Duncan and J. Howell (eds) *Structural Adjustment and the African Farmer*. London: Overseas Development Institute.

Devereux, S. 1993. *Theories of Famine*. New York: Harvester Wheatsheaf.

Devereux, S. 1999. 'Transfers and Safety Nets' in S. Devereux (ed.) *Food Security in Africa: A Reader* (forthcoming).

Drèze, J. and Sen, A. 1989. *Hunger and Public Action*. Oxford: Clarendon Press.

Easter, Christopher 1999. 'Small States Development: a Commonwealth Vulnerability Index', *The Round Table* 351: 403 – 22.

Ellis, F. 1993. 'Food Security and Stabilisation of Rice Prices in Indonesia', in P. Berck and D. Pigman (eds) *Food Security and Food Inventories in Developing Countries*. Wallingford: CAB International.

Ellis, F.; Magrath, W. and Trotter, B. 1991. 'Indonesian Rice Marketing Study (1989 – 91: Final Report)', Report No REP/CON/52, BULOG/NRI Development Project, Jakarta.

FAO 1996. *State of Food and Agriculture 1996* (FAOSTAT TS software by the United States Department of Agriculture). Rome: Food and Agriculture Organization of the United Nations.

FAO 1998. *State of Food and Agriculture 1998* (FAOSTAT TS software by the United States Department of Agriculture). Rome: Food and Agriculture Organization of the United Nations.

FAO 1999a. 'The Agreement on Agriculture: some preliminary assessment from the experience so far'. Paper presented at the conference 'The Uruguay Round Agreement on Agriculture: Taking Stock', sponsored by CIIR/UK Food Group, Westminster Hall, London, 28 January 1999, by Panos Konandreas, Ramesh Sharma and Jim Greenfield.

FAO 1999b. 'Some issues that may arise in the continuation of the reform process in agriculture'. Paper presented at a Round Table on Follow Up to the Uruguay Round Agreement on Agriculture, New Delhi, India, 18 – 19 January 1999, by Panos Konandreas, Ramesh Sharma and Jim Greenfield.

FAO 1999c. 'Supporting import-competing agricultural sectors with tariffs, safeguards and domestic measures within the framework of the Uruguay Round Agreements'. Paper presented at a Round Table on Follow Up to the Uruguay Round Agreement on Agriculture, New Delhi, India, 18 – 19 January 1999, by Ramesh Sharma and Panos Konandreas.

FAO 1999d. *FAOSTAT Data* (website: http://apps.fao.org/cgi-bin/nph-db.pl). Rome: Food and Agriculture Organization of the United Nations.

Gaiha, R. 1993. 'Design of Poverty Alleviation Strategies', *FAO Economic and Social Development Paper*, No 115. Rome: Food and Agriculture Organization of the United Nations.

GATT 1994. The Results of the Uruguay Round of Multilateral Trade Negotiations. Geneva: GATT Secretariat.

Goldin, I. and Knudsen, O. (eds) 1990. *Agricultural Trade Liberalization: Implications for Developing Countries*. Paris: OECD/The World Bank.

Goldin, I. and van der Mensbrugghe, D. 1992. 'Trade liberalisation: what's at stake?', *Policy Brief*. Paris: OECD Development Centre.

Goldin, I., Knudsen, O. and van der Mensbrugghe, D. 1993. *Trade Liberalisation: Global Economic Implications*. Paris: OECD/The World Bank.

Green, R. 1994. 'Production by Poor People', *IDS Bulletin*, 24(3): July.

Harriss, B. 1992. *Child Nutrition and Poverty in South India*. New Delhi: Concept Publishing Company.

Hazell, P. and Roell, A. 1983. 'Rural Growth Linkages: Household Expenditure Patterns in Malaysia and Nigeria', *Research Report* No 41. Washington DC: International Food Policy Research Institute.

Humphrey, J. and Schmitz, H. 1996. 'The Triple C Approach to Local Industrial Policy', *World Development*, 24(12).

IBRD 1986. *Poverty and Hunger: Issues and Options for Food Security in Developing Countries*. Washington DC: The World Bank.

IBRD 1990. *World Development Report*. Washington DC: The World Bank.

IBRD 1994. *Industrial Structures and the Development of Small and Medium Enterprise Linkages: Examples from East Asia*. Washington DC: The World Bank.

IFPRI 1992. *Improving Food Security of the Poor*. Washington DC: International Food Policy Research Institute.

IMF 1997. *Government Finance Statistics Yearbook 1997*. Washington DC: International Monetary Fund.

ITC 1997. *The SME and the Global Market Place*. Geneva: International Trade Centre.

Jayne, T. and Chisvo, M. 1991. 'Unravelling Zimbabwe's food insecurity paradox', *Food Policy*, 16(4).

MALDM 1988 – 93. Reports of Catchment Approach Planning and Rapid Catchment Analysis. Soil and Water Conservation Branch, Ministry of Agriculture, Livestock Development and Marketing, Nairobi, Kenya.

Maxwell, S. 1990. 'Food Security in Developing Countries: Issues and Options for the 1990s', *IDS Bulletin*, 21(3): July.

Maxwell, S. 1999. 'The Evolution of Thinking about Food Security', in S. Devereux (ed.) *Food Security in Africa: A Reader* (forthcoming).

Mellor, J. 1986. 'Agriculture on the Road to Industrialization', in J. Lewis and V. Kallab (eds) 'Development Strategies Reconsidered', *Third World Policy Perspectives* No 5. New Brunswick, NJ: Transaction Books for the Overseas Development Council.

Mukherjee, A. 1994. *Structural Adjustment Programmes and Food Security*. Aldershot: Avebury.

Page, S., Davenport, M. and Hewitt, A. 1991. 'The GATT Uruguay Round: effects on developing countries', *ODI Special Report*. London: Overseas Development Institute.

Pinckney, T. 1993. 'Storage, trade and price policies for maize in Southern Africa', *Food Policy*: August.

Pinstrup-Anderson, P. 1989. *Government Policy, Food Security and Nutrition in Sub-Saharan Africa*. Ithaca, NY: The Programme.

Pretty, J.N. and Chambers, R. 1994. 'Towards a learning paradigm: new professionalism and institutions for a sustainable agriculture', in I. Scoones and J. Thompson (eds) *Beyond Farmer First*. London: IT Publications.

Pretty, J.N.; Thompson, J. and Kiara, J. 1994. 'Agricultural Regeneration in Kenya: the Catchment Approach to Soil and Water Conservation', *Ambio: a Journal of the Human Environment*. Royal Swedish Academy of Sciences.

Pryke, J. and Woodward, D. 1994. 'The GATT Agreement on Agriculture: will it help developing countries', *CIIR Briefing Paper*. London: Catholic Institute for International Relations.

Ratnam, C. 1991. 'Institutions for Promoting Technological Modernisation of Indian Small Enterprises', in A. Bhalla (ed.) *Small and Medium Enterprises: Technology Policies and Options*. New York: Greenwood Press.

Ravallion, M. and Datt, G. 1995. 'Is Targeting through a Work Requirement Efficient?: Some Evidence for Rural India', in D. van der Walle and K. Nead (eds) *Public Spending and the Poor: Theory and Evidence*. Washington DC: The World Bank.

Rukuni, M. and Jayne, T. 1995. *Alleviating Hunger in Zimbabwe: Towards a National Food Security Strategy*. Harare: University of Zimbabwe Publications.

Scoones, I. 1998a. 'Sustainable Rural Livelihoods: A Framework for Analysis', *Working Paper* No. 72. Brighton: Institute of Development Studies.

Scoones, I. 1998b. Agricultural Research and Extension: seminar given at the Institute of Development Studies, October 1998.

Sen, A. 1981. *Poverty and Famines*. New York: Oxford University Press.

Sen, A. 1986. 'The Causes of Famine: A Reply', *Food Policy*, 11.

Sijm, J. 1997. *Food Security and Policy Interventions in Sub-Saharan Africa: Lessons from the Past Two Decades*. Amsterdam: Thesis Publishers.

Stevens, C.; Kennan, J. and Yates, J. 1998. 'Levelling the field: will CAP reform provide a fair deal for developing countries?, *CIIR Discussion Paper*. London: Catholic Institute for International Relations.

Swinbank, A.; Jordan, K. and Beard, N. 1999. 'Implications for Developing Countries of Likely Reforms of the Common Agricultural Policy of the European Union', report prepared for the Economic Affairs Division of the Commonwealth Secretariat. London: Commonwealth Secretariat.

UNCTAD/WIDER 1990. *Agricultural Trade Liberalisation in the Uruguay Round: Implications for Developing Countries*. Geneva: United Nations.

van der Walle, D. 1995. 'Incidence and Targeting: An Overview of Implications for Research and Policy', in D. van der Walle and K. Nead (eds) *Public Spending and the Poor: Theory and Evidence*. Washington DC: The World Bank.

Woodward, D. 1995. 'Structural Adjustment, Cash Crops and Food Security', *Appropriate Technology*, 22(3): December.

WTO 1996. *The Results of the Uruguay Round* (CD-Rom). Geneva: World Trade Organization.

Recent Commonwealth Secretariat Economic Publications

Commonwealth Economic Papers

David Greenway and Chris Milner, *The Uruguay Round and Developing Countries: An Assessment*, No.25, 1996

Michael Davenport, *The Uruguay Round and NAFTA: The Challenge for Commonwealth Caribbean Countries*, No.26, 1996

Economic Affairs Division, *Money Laundering: Key Issues and Possible* Action, No.27, 1997

David Pearce and Ece Ozdemiroglu, *Integrating the Economy and the Environment – Policy and Practice*, No.28, 1997

Robert Cassen, *Strategies for Growth and Poverty Alleviation*, No.29, 1997

Richard Portes and David Vines, *Coping with International Capital Flows*, No.30, 1997

Sanjaya Lall, *Attracting Foreign Direct Investment*, No. 31, 1997

M. McQueen, C. Phillips, D. Hallam & A.Swinbank, *ACP-EU Trade and Aid Co-operation Post-Lomé IV*, No.32, 1998

Sanjaya Lall and Ganeshan Wignaraja, *Mauritius: Dynamising Export Competitiveness*, No.33, 1998.

Report of a Commonwealth Working Group, *Promoting Private Capital Flows and Handling Volatility:Role of National and International Policies*, No.34, 1998

Gerry K. Helleiner, *Private Capital Flows and Development: The Role of National and International Policies*, No.35, 1998

Joseph L.S. Abbey, *The Political Process and Management of Economic Change*, No.36, 1998

Christopher Stevens, Mathew McQueen and Jane Kennan: *After Lome IV: A strategy for ACP-EU Relations in the 21st Century*, No.37, 2000

Alan Swinbank, Kate Jordan and Nick Beard, *Implications for Developing Countries of likely Reforms of the Common Agricultural Policy of the European Union*, No.38, 2000

Sanjaya Lall, *Promoting Industrial Competitiveness in Developing Countries: Lessons from Asia*, No.39, 1999

Jonathan P. Atkins, Sonia Mazzi, Christopher D. Easter, *A Commonwealth Vulnerability Index for Developing Countries: The Position of Small States*, No.40, 2000

Montek S. Ahluwalia, *Reforming the Global Financial Architecture*, No.41, 2000

To order these or any other publication, please contact:
Publications Unit, Commonwealth Secretariat, Marlborough House,
Pall Mall, London SW1Y 5HX, United Kingdom
Tel: +44 (0)20 7747 6342; or Fax: +44 (0)20 7839 9081